100 Tips For Bass Guitar
You Should Have Been Told

D1601934

Printed and bound in Great Britain by Antony Rowe Limited, Chippenham, Wiltshire

Published in the UK by SMT, an imprint of Sanctuary Publishing Limited, Sanctuary House, 45–53 Sinclair Road, London W14 0NS, United Kingdom

www.sanctuarypublishing.com

All quotes kindly provided by *Bass Guitar* magazine

ISBN: 1-84492-004-6

100 Tips For Bass Guitar
You Should Have Been Told

Stuart Clayton

smt

ACKNOWLEDGEMENTS

Thanks to Kevin Beardsley for the recording, Simon Tucker for programming, Syd Harris, Bernie Goodfellow for his superb basses, Keith Kerslake, Martin Greenlee, Mansons, *Bass Guitar* magazine and my students.

Extra-special thanks to Adrian Ashton for guidance, being a fellow bass nut and for lending me so many basses!

Finally, thanks to all of my friends and family, particularly my rather wonderful parents.

On the CD, Stuart Clayton used a GB Guitars Rumour bass and EBS amplification for this recording. Strings were by Elite. Drum programming by Simon Tucker.

CD recorded, compiled and produced by Kevin Beardsley, April 2003.

Web/info: www.stuartclayton.co.uk

BOOK CONTENTS

CD CONTENTS

FOREWORD

I hope you enjoy this book – I certainly enjoyed putting it together for you. The aim is to introduce you to some new techniques and to teach you a little about the history of our favourite instrument. I also hope that I've been able to present some music theory to you in a sensible manner and one that you can understand. If, however, you have any questions or comments, you can reach me through my website, www.stuartclayton.co.uk – I will do my best to help!

Stuart Clayton
Spring 2003

INTRODUCTION

No doubt you already know that playing the bass, or indeed any instrument, can be a very rewarding experience. You probably also know that at other times it can be extremely daunting and frustrating, so much so that some days it seems easier just to give up. With so many styles, techniques and songs out there, it's often difficult to know what to focus on, what to learn and, more importantly, what to play. If this sounds familiar, then this book is for you.

I like to think of music as being one big jigsaw puzzle, even if sometimes it seems that it's one of those unfathomable 10,000-piece ones. Like a jigsaw, it often takes some searching to find the piece you want, but when you *do* find that elusive piece it can connect you to another, or even link a couple of sections together for you. Then things start to make sense. That's also the aim of this book – to help you to understand the many different aspects of playing and studying the bass. By doing so, it will help you to put the whole puzzle together and become the player that you want to be. Of course, becoming that player will mean something different for each person reading this.

What Do You Want From The Bass?

That's the first question you need to ask yourself. I've taught many people who have learnt their instrument to a reasonable standard only to find that they don't know where to go with it next. They play the same licks over and over again, they don't learn anything new, and they start to bore themselves with it – they know there's a bigger picture, but they can't seem to focus on the bits they need to help them see it. Some even give up. If you feel like your playing is stuck in a rut, hopefully this book will show you what's missing and help you to get out of it, because once you know what you want from your instrument, you can then begin to work towards seeing the whole picture – or jigsaw. You can start to use your time more wisely, set your own goals based on this and be happier for it. Goals are very important for a musician, and we'll talk more about them

in a minute. Some of you will have a voracious appetite for knowledge and will want to learn everything you can and pursue a musical career. That's great news, and I wish you luck. Hopefully you'll find something of use to you within these pages, even if it's just a new way of looking at something you know already. Or maybe you're the type of player who just wants to learn some new techniques so you can play along with your favourite albums. Again, there should be plenty here for you here, and maybe along the way you'll even pick up some other pieces of that jigsaw you didn't even know you wanted. Finally, even if you're a total beginner, there is a place for you here. This book might deal with some fairly tricky concepts along with the more obvious material, but I promise you that along the way I'm going to be doing my best to explain everything in a way that you can understand.

Goals, Big And Small

Goals are very useful for a musician. Once you know the kind of player you want to be, you can work towards achieving that goal. This is best done by creating a practice schedule for yourself. I'm always keen to promote the virtues of practising and Chapter 5, 'Practising', is devoted entirely to this subject. However, a common mistake made by musicians is setting unreasonable goals – effectively biting off more than they can chew. Start simply, with targets you know you'll be able to meet. It's entirely possible for you to learn to play like Flea, Jaco Pastorius or Fieldy, but to do so you must take small steps – they had to.

Let's look at it a different way. If you were to decide you wanted to learn to play snooker, for example, you wouldn't expect to get a 147 break on day one, would you? No, you'd build up to that – you'd work on your potting, study the angles, work on your game and basically take the whole thing in smaller steps. You'd have to, otherwise you'd just be setting yourself up for a lot of disappointment.

It's exactly the same with music. Setting yourself large,

ambitious goals will result in failure more often than not, and this in turn will lead to disillusionment. We don't want that, so let's look at learning to play in small, manageable chunks. If you set yourself a reasonable goal, one that you know you'll be able to achieve with a little work, then you *will* achieve it. And you'll feel great for doing so. You'll then be able to set yourself another goal – you'll feel great when you achieve that one as well. Progressing like this, in smaller increments, will get you where you want to be without too much disappointment.

What You Put In...

As with any instrument, you get out of the bass what you put in. The more time you spend honing your craft, the better at it you'll become. There will be some hard work ahead, but that doesn't mean it can't be enjoyable – after all, we're all playing the bass because we enjoy it, right? As I explain in Chapter 5, practice is the key to your success, and with enough of this you can do anything you like. Keep that in mind when things get tough. All of the players that you admire today had to spend years perfecting their technique and learning their instrument, and I'm afraid you're going to have to as well.

Hero Syndrome

Here's a common scenario: quite frequently students come to me wanting to play like their heroes, whoever they might be. Usually it's the bass player from whatever band happens to be the flavour of the month, and that's fine – I was exactly the same. My hero (one of many) was Mark King, and when I was younger all I wanted was to be able to play like him, so I practised the bass until finally I could – it took a long time. The trouble was, when I got there, I couldn't play much else. Obviously, I wasn't a great deal of use to anyone unless they wanted to play Level 42 covers, which invariably they didn't. If I wanted to get work as a bass player, I knew I had to go back and learn all the stuff I had missed out along the way. So I studied the other bass players I liked – Jaco Pastorius, Stanley Clarke, Gene Simmons, Jack Bruce, Duck Dunn, James Jamerson and many others. I learnt a lot and began to see music as a whole picture, or jigsaw, rather than just the small part of it I had chosen. This helped me become a much more rounded bass player with my own sound. But I got the feeling that I had taken the long way round. By telling you this, hopefully you'll avoid making the same mistake.

My point is that, while it's okay to emulate your favourite player, you should try to keep an open mind. You don't have to play exactly like them, play the same

bass and wear it as they do. Try to be yourself. Play how you feel comfortable. Many students have come to me with a very narrow view of bass playing. They've found the style and player that they like and that's what they want to play. Fine – that's what I teach them. But as a trade-off, for every song they learn in that style, I ask them to learn a song of my choosing, something completely different. More often than not, they grow to like this new style I've introduced to them and are excited by it because it's not one that would have occurred to them naturally. As a teacher, it's very rewarding to see a student realise what else is out there and the possibilities it offers them.

Finally...

This book is divided up into three sections. The first part contains information about the music theory that will be relevant to you as a bass guitarist. As with all the subjects covered herein, I have attempted to present the information in an easy-to-digest format – hopefully you'll find it an easy and informative read. The first chapter of this section also contains a detailed history of the bass for those of you who want to know a little more about it.

The second section focuses on left- and right-hand technique. This is where we look at strengthening up your left hand and developing finger independence. If that sounds a little boring, you'll be pleased to hear that this is also where you'll find the chapters on slap bass, fingerstyle and playing with a pick. I've written an overview of each technique, which should get you started or help you to improve on what you already know.

The final section is a selection of chapters on topics that are perhaps not essential to you as a bassist but which you will still find helpful.

Where appropriate I've recorded some of the examples on the accompanying CD to demonstrate how they should sound – I hope you find this useful. You will see a CD icon near the relevant part of the text which also gives you the track number.

Finally, this isn't one of those books that you're meant to read from cover to cover. You can if you want to, but I don't recommend it. The idea is that you dip into it when you want to know about something. Experienced players will probably have no interest in reading Chapter 2, 'Tuning Up', but might get something from the one of the techniques chapters. Equally, a beginner isn't going to dive straight in on the chapters on scales but is more likely to want that chapter on tuning. The information is here to be digested at your leisure as and when you want. Whatever you do, enjoy it.

1 THE EVOLUTION OF THE ELECTRIC BASS

'Remember that the number one job of a bassist is to make everyone else sound good!'
Dave Pomeroy, Nashville session bassist

Although it has been around for just over 50 years, in comparison to the piano the electric bass is still a young instrument. When Leo Fender introduced his Precision bass to the world in 1951, it was with the intention of getting the bass player to be heard. Prior to the electric bass, the bottom end was held down by upright basses – large, unwieldy instruments that were difficult to play in tune and even more difficult to amplify.

Using the template he had already created for the electric guitar, Leo Fender and his business partner, George Fullerton, set about improving the bassists' lot, creating an electric instrument that could easily be amplified and that had frets, thereby enabling the bassist to play precisely in tune, hence the term Precision bass. Although their 34-inch-scale electric bass was no doubt a revolutionary design, I can't imagine that even in his wildest dreams Leo Fender knew just how successful the electric bass would be, nor how it would grow and develop over the years. Since its humble inception, the electric bass has enabled the bass player not only to play a stronger and more supportive role (not to mention a more audible one!) in the rhythm section but also to evolve into a soloist in his/her own right.

Once the concept of an electric bass began to grow in popularity, other guitar manufacturers began to follow suit and started to produce bass guitars of their own. In the late '50s, Rickenbacker produced the first through-neck electric bass, including a feature that is very prominent in the design of today's electric basses. Gibson, a company already famous for its electric guitars, began to produce basses, most notably the EB-3 and, in the '60s, the Thunderbird.

Meanwhile, throughout the decade, Fender continued to fine-tune their Precision bass design and also introduced the Fender Jazz bass. The Fender Jazz sported a slimmer neck, a more ergonomic body design and two pick-ups. But while the design of the electric bass itself was exceptional, it was the bass players that made music on it that elevated it to the level of popularity that it enjoys today.

The '60s brought with them a whole host of bassists whose playing began to redefine the role of the instrument. The most notable of these has to be James Jamerson, an upright-bass player from Detroit who switched to electric and became the player who many consider to be the electric bass's first true innovator. Jamerson played a 1962 Precision bass and anchored most of the hit songs that came out of the Motown hit factory in the '60s and early '70s. Using just one right-hand finger to pluck the strings, Jamerson's bass parts brought the songs on which he played to life with his use of 16th-note lines, syncopations, chromatic passing tones and unrivalled groove. Through his work with artists such as Stevie Wonder, Marvin Gaye, The Supremes, The Marvelettes and Jr Walker And The All Stars, Jamerson created lines that not only got people dancing (a big part of a bass player's job!) but that also inspired and continue to inspire every other bassist who heard them.

One player who was notably inspired by Jamerson was Paul McCartney. Playing a Hofner violin bass for much of his time with The Beatles, McCartney's lines in the early 1960s started out relatively simple. However, by the time the band recorded *Sgt Pepper's Lonely Heart's Club Band* in 1967, McCartney had grown as a bass player and was producing stunningly effective, melodic bass lines that had become an integral part of the Beatles sound. Tracks like 'Something', 'Lovely Rita', 'Hey Bulldog' and 'Lucy In The Sky With Diamonds' are an education in supportive, melodic bass playing – a fact that still holds true today.

McCartney also used the bass to lead the song, as illustrated on the wonderful 'Come Together' from the *Abbey Road* album. Like Jamerson with the Motown record label, McCartney was able to reach millions of people with his playing due to his status as the bassist in the world's most famous band. Awareness and popularity of the instrument was beginning to grow rapidly.

Alongside Jamerson and McCartney were a whole host

of bass players who had heartily embraced the instrument. Among these were Carol Kaye, Duck Dunn, Tommy Cogbill, Jerry Jemmott, John Entwistle and Jack Bruce. Bruce, another Jamerson-inspired bassist, brought a previously unseen level of improvisation to rock music with the band Cream, while John Entwistle, with The Who, was developing his own unique technique and creating lines and solos that set a new standard for the rock bassist. John's bass parts on classic Who tracks such as 'Won't Get Fooled Again' and 'The Real Me' are unforgettable, as are his inspired solo bursts on 'My Generation'. It was undoubtedly in the '60s that the bassists' role began to change, evolving from being a purely supportive and rather unadventurous background instrument to one that could be innovative and inspiring while retaining the supportive element.

As the '60s progressed, the first valid attempts were made to expand upon the design of the original Fender bass. In 1966, Fender came up with the first five-string bass, although unlike today's five-string instruments it featured a high C rather than a low B. Unfortunately for Fender, it was not a successful venture and was not embraced by the bass-playing community.

Alembic had considerably more success in 1969 when they began to produce the first basses with active electronics. This proved to be a big success and the idea spread. Today all high-range basses and an increasingly large number of low-range basses feature active electronics.

The '70s also saw some major innovations in the design of the instrument, not least being the arrival of the first five-string bass as we know it today. In 1975, inspired by the rather obscure five-string upright basses used occasionally by orchestral players, session man Jimmy Johnson decided to customise a five-string Alembic (which had a high C) to include a low B string, which he had had custom-made. The result was a success, and the first five-string bass was born. It would, however, be another decade or so before the idea really took off.

In 1978, the Alembic company began to experiment with constructing necks out of carbon fibre (also known as graphite) as an alternative to wood. Carbon fibre is a very strong and very light material, which made building instrument necks out of it a shrewd innovation. Mould-breaking though it was, though, like the five-string bass, the idea did not catch on immediately.

While the design of the bass was developing and improving, the '70s also saw the arrival of a new wave of revolutionary bass players. First and foremost of these was Jaco Pastorius, who in 1976 released his first solo album and created a point that would forever after divide the history of the instrument into 'Before Jaco' and 'After Jaco'

periods. Jaco brought to the bass an outstanding level of musicality based on years of gigging with funk and soul bands in the Florida area. Playing a de-fretted Fender Jazz, Jaco was tirelessly able to play 16th-note grooves that were melodic and funky as well as being supportive, building on and going beyond what Jamerson had done before. Once again, the supportive nature of the instrument was being redefined – and that was just for starters.

Jaco was also a master of jazz harmony and was able to play fluidly through complex jazz changes, soloing with the grace and facility of any sax player. The opening track on his 1976 self-titled debut album, *Donna Lee*, still sets the standard against which any bass soloist is judged today. He also brought new meaning to the technique of playing harmonics on the bass. Previously used only as a method for tuning the bass, Jaco took harmonics and combined them with his intricate chordal knowledge to create voicings and lines that were beyond the limits of anything previously heard on the bass guitar. The track 'Portrait Of Tracy' is a wonderful example of this and remains to this day an education in bass harmonics. More importantly, it's also a beautiful piece of music.

Jaco continued to innovate with the jazz-fusion band Weather Report, most notably with his artificial-harmonics melody line on 'Birdland', his beautiful fretless work on 'A Remark You Made' and his stunning soloing agility on tracks such as 'Havona' and 'Port Of Entry', all of which justly earned him the title of The World's Greatest Bass Player.

Although Jaco arguably led the bass movement of the '70s, he wasn't alone. In the early part of the decade, Larry Graham began to make a name for himself with his pioneering 'thump-and-pluck' technique, commonly referred to today as *slap bass*. This involves thumping the string with the thumb of the right hand and plucking with the first or second fingers to create a percussive feel. With his groundbreaking work with Sly And The Family Stone and Graham Central Station, Larry Graham changed funk bass forever, creating a technique that in itself would influence bassists all over the world from that point onwards. Through listening to tracks like 'Hair' by Graham Central Station and 'Thank You' by Sly And The Family Stone, the impact that Graham had on the bass is clear. Today, he is still regarded as the innovator of slap bass and continues to inspire and create, particularly in his work with The Artist.

Alongside Jaco and Larry was Stanley Clarke, who, like Jaco, brought an awareness of jazz to his playing and was one of the first players to double successfully as a soloist and sideman on both electric and upright basses. Stanley's work with Return To Forever and Chick Corea has secured him a place in the list of all-time greats, and tracks like

'School Days' and 'Lopsy Lu' are required listening for any bassist. To this day he remains one of the true innovators.

But it wasn't just in the world of jazz and fusion that advances were being made. Things were also changing in the rock arena with players like Geezer Butler (Black Sabbath) and Gene Simmons (KISS) making a lot of noise both metaphorically and sonically speaking. Both players used plectrums and had strong song-based melodic sense that came directly from the Jamerson/McCartney era. Since their groups both had (and still have) enormous worldwide followings, their bass work reached and inspired a lot of young ears.

The same was happening in the UK, where bassist John Paul Jones was bringing the instrument to the ears of the masses with the rock band Led Zeppelin. As one of rock music's true innovators, Jones combined blues and rock influences to create powerful lines that permeated the band's heavy-metal sound and set a new standard for rock/heavy-metal bass playing.

As the '80s arrived, the bass continued to evolve. Active electronics became more prevalent and the number of luthiers turning out quality instruments increased. Ken Smith, a New York-based luthier, began to build five-string basses and at the behest of renowned session bassist Anthony Jackson built several six-string basses tuned B, E, A, D, G, C. Originally built as 34-inch-scale instruments with narrow string spacing, the design was eventually refined to Jackson's specifications to include wide string spacing, as found on a standard four-string bass, and a longer scale length.

Universal acceptance of the six string bass was still some time off, but the five-string was growing in popularity and continued to do so throughout the '80s. In the early part of the decade, the concept of graphite necks also began to grow in popularity, helped along in no small part by Status in the UK and Alembic, Steinberger and Modulus in the US. Steinberger and Status used graphite extensively, with both companies eventually developing basses made entirely of the material.

Just as the '70s had seen a dramatic bass movement, the '80s followed suit, with several bassists stepping forward to take the instrument to new levels. One such bassist was Mark King, who with Level 42 helped re-ignite the Britfunk movement in the early '80s. King took what Larry Graham and Stanley Clarke had already done with the slap-bass technique and took it further still, creating a percussive yet melodic 16th-note slap style that underpinned many of the band's tracks. As frontman for Level 42, who achieved huge chart success in the mid-'80s, King attracted musicians to the bass in their thousands with a slap

technique that was almost as visually impressive as it sounded. Aside from revolutionising the bassist's role within the band, King was one of the key players in boosting the popularity of Trace Elliot, a UK-based bass-amplifier manufacturer that was one of the first to introduce the 4x10 cabinet that we take for granted today.

While King was busy reinventing the bass in the UK, Marcus Miller was doing the same in the US, being one of the first bassists to write commercially successful bass-orientated solo albums. Marcus developed fearsome slap chops as well as a mastery of jazz soloing and grooving, making him a force to be reckoned with. Combined with his skills as a writer, producer, arranger and bandleader, it seems that in Marcus we have the perfect example of how the bass player's role has expanded since Leo Fender invented the electric bass.

Other leading figures in the '80s bass evolution were Billy Sheehan, Tony Levin and Pino Palladino. Sheehan spent years developing a tapping technique inspired by the genius of guitar virtuoso Eddie Van Halen. When he hit the big-time in the mid-'80s, as bassist in Dave Lee Roth's band, the rock world watched in wonder as he exchanged rapid-fire solo tapping flurries with guitarist Steve Vai. Up until this point, tapping had been almost purely the domain of guitarists, but Sheehan not only proved that it could be done on a bass; he proved that it could be a valid and exciting technique and used it to enhance his strong rock-groove foundation.

Tony Levin also made the public sit up and take notice with his work with Peter Gabriel and King Crimson. Aside from his strong four-string work, Levin doubled on the Chapman Stick, a guitar/bass hybrid played in a two-handed tapping style. He also developed a very funky technique of using drumsticks attached to his fingers to play the instrument. I think it's unlikely that Leo Fender ever envisaged *that* happening...

As the bass moved into the '90s, the five-string became more and more prominent, gradually reaching the position it enjoys today as an integral part of any professional bassist's arsenal. Bass players – particularly those on the jazz/fusion scene – were slowly coming to accept the six-string bass as well, with John Patittucci and Anthony Jackson being just a couple of the players to be using it as a main instrument. There was also a significant increase in the number of bass luthiers, and today a quick flick through the pages of any bass magazine will reveal a growing number of quality instrument makers offering their own take on the bass guitar.

One of the main exponents of the bass on the '90s popular-music scene was Flea. With The Red Hot Chili

Peppers, Flea had developed a super-funky slap style that was at the forefront of the band's sound and which can be heard in abundance in any of the band's output from the '80s. However, with the release of the *BloodSugarSexMagik* album in 1991, Flea introduced the world to a more restrained side of his playing. While still undoubtedly funky, Flea's sparse Parliament-inspired bass parts oozed sophistication with their subtlety and strong sense of groove. They became the bass parts for any young bassist to learn and remain so today.

Flea was not alone in bringing the bass to young ears in the '90s since he had help from another bass heavyweight in Les Claypool of Primus. Claypool based his rock-funk trio around his manic and quirky bass playing, which was as amazing as his ability to sing effortlessly nonsensical lyrics over the top of it!

However, after the big-hair guitar-trickery bands of the '80s, things were changing, and the beginning of the '90s saw the arrival of grunge. Just as punk had been a breath of fresh air at the end of the '70s, grunge took everything that was complex about '80s rock music and disregarded it, shifting the focus from manic guitar and bass solos to ultra-simple parts that supported the music and left ample room for the attitudes and stage presence of the performers. The key exponents of the grunge movement were undoubtedly Nirvana, who with their biggest single, 'Smells Like Teen Spirit', gave the world one of the simplest and catchiest bass parts in rock history.

In spite of its simplicity – or more likely because of it – the grunge movement was still important in the evolution of the bass guitar, reminding bassists that it wasn't necessary to be over-complicated in order to create an effective bass part. Other notable figures of the grunge style were The Stone Temple Pilots, Soundgarden and Pearl Jam, featuring Robert DeLeo, Ben Shepherd and Jeff Ament on bass respectively.

While things were undoubtedly getting simpler in the rock world, this wasn't the case in jazz/fusion music. A new wave of bass virtuosos was emerging, artists who applied techniques that were expanding the boundaries of the instrument even further. Players like Michael Manring, Steve Bailey, Gary Willis and Oteil Burbridge were building on the standard that Jaco set and were taking the concept of the bass as a solo instrument further still. Victor Wooten was also busy raising the bar for slap players with his astonishing double-thumb technique. The keys to Wooten's success, in addition to his jaw-dropping technique, are his ability to groove and his strong melodic sense and musicality, crucial elements for every bass player to master.

In the mid '90s there was a sudden surge in the popularity of home computers and the Internet, and this has also had positive effects on bass players and musicians in general. Most groups and bass players now have their own web sites, and there are also online forums where you can discuss the instrument you love with people all over the world. Meanwhile, learning your favourite song has become easier thanks to the number of computer-savvy musicians uploading tablature, sheet music, MP3s and MIDI files. As publishers get wise to the new bass-playing trend, more instructional books, DVDs and videos have become available than ever before. There has never been more material available to help you become a better bass player.

Now, in the 21st century, the bass continues to grow and evolve – as it always will. Many of the players mentioned in this chapter are still going strong and continue to amaze us with their playing. In recent years, as rock has come back into favour and evolved into nu metal, there are more young bassists out there making a name for themselves and encouraging more young players to pick up the bass. The bass is no longer the 'uncool' instrument in the group and one you get lumbered with if your guitar playing isn't up to scratch. The role of the bass player has become more important than ever before. Hopefully, in having read this chapter, you will see why – maybe you'll be one of the ones to take it further still.

2 TUNING UP

'Players are less capable of manipulating their instrument of choice than they have ever been.
A tuner has replaced their ear.' *Jeff Berlin*

There are several different ways to tune the bass, and when you find one that you like you'll most probably stick with it. Basses are quite reliable since, for the most part, they stay reasonably in tune when you're not using them. However, every time you pick up the bass to play, you should check the tuning. If you keep your bass in either a soft or a hard case, it's entirely possible that a tuning peg will have been moved, and this is also true if you leave the bass leaning against a wall. The safest option is to buy a guitar stand, which will enable the bass to stand freely without the tuning pegs coming into contact with anything.

However you tune up, you must always have something that will provide you with an accurate reference pitch – unless you're lucky enough to have perfect pitch! Assuming that you don't, a reference pitch can be either a keyboard (or other instrument that is reliably in tune) or an electronic guitar tuner. An electronic tuner is an excellent purchase for any bassist/guitarist, as it is never wrong and will enable you to tune up on stage without amplifying the bass – perfect for those function gigs! A tuner such as this can be purchased from your local music shop for as little as £15 ($23).

Warning! Tuning without a reference pitch can result in an instrument that's in tune with itself but not with anything else – not much good for playing with other musicians! There is a reference pitch of G on Track 4 of the accompanying CD.

There are three ways that I am aware of for tuning the bass, which I will illustrate for you here. All are accepted methods and it really doesn't matter which you use.

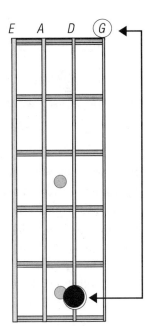

Method 1

▲ Track 5

Firstly, make sure you have the top string (G) of your bass in tune – check with a reference pitch, as mentioned above, before proceeding any further.

Now play the open G string and the fifth fret of the D string – also a G. Both positions should produce the same pitch, indicating that the strings are in tune with each other.

If the pitches are not identical, adjust the D string's tuning key until they are. Here's a particularly important point: make sure that you adjust the correct tuning peg. If you accidentally adjust the G-string tuning peg, your only in-tune string will now be out of tune!

The two diagrams at the top of the next page illustrate how to get the rest of the strings in tune. Repeat the previous process with the open D string and the fifth fret on the A string. Again, both should produce the same pitch – in this case, a D.

Once more, repeat the process with the open A string and the fifth fret on the E string. Both should produce the same pitch – an A.

The bass should now be in tune. Try playing a few lines to see how it sounds. If anything sounds amiss, check each note pairing as illustrated to find the fault. Bear in mind that small mistakes are cumulative and will be even more obvious by the time you finish tuning! You'll be able to hear each of these note pairings on Track 5 of the CD:

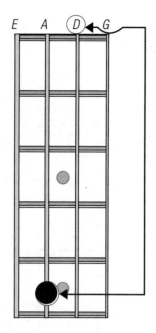
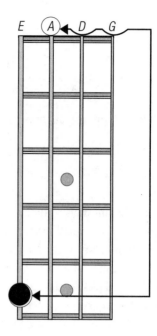

Method 2

Track 6

Method 2 is another very commonly used method for tuning and is for the slightly more advanced player. It is similar to Method 1 except that it uses harmonics. Harmonics are played by placing a finger over the fret without pushing it down and then playing the string. This will produce a bell-like tone that is above the usual bass register. One of the advantages of using this method is that you don't need to keep your finger on the string to keep the harmonic ringing, enabling you to have your left hand free to manipulate the tuning peg. I find this method of tuning more accurate than the previous one. You will see why shortly.

As before, you must ensure that you have the G string in tune before tuning the other strings, so check out the reference pitch on Track 4 of the CD. Once you're happy with the tuning of your G string, play the harmonic at the seventh fret on the G string and the harmonic at the fifth fret on the D string. They should be identical.

You'll notice that harmonic notes aren't always the same pitches as their fretted brothers. While the seventh-fret G-string harmonic is a D – like its fretted note – the fifth-fret D-string harmonic is also a D, while its fretted companion is a G. This isn't something you need to worry about right now, as long as the two harmonics sound the same.

If the harmonics aren't in tune with each other, you'll hear a 'pulse' in the sound, a movement that slows down the closer towards being in tune the two notes become. If you can hear this pulsing, slowly tune upwards or downwards until the pulsing is inaudible (Track 6 on the CD illustrates this). This is the main advantage this method has over the first. For those of you who play five-string basses, you'll find it much easier to tune up that difficult low B string using this method.

Next repeat the procedure down a string, playing the harmonic at the seventh fret on the D string and the fifth fret on the A string. Again, they should be identical:

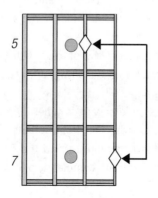
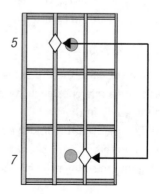

And again with the seventh fret on the A string and the fifth fret on the E string:

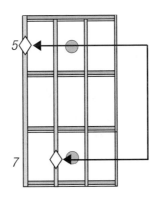

Your bass should now be in tune. Check for inconsistencies and correct them as necessary. Again, be careful to get each string right as you go, as small mistakes add up!

Method 3

Method 3 involves the use of a combination of harmonics and open strings and is a little more advanced. Once again, tune your open G string to the reference pitch on Track 4. Now play the open G string and compare it to the harmonic at the 12th fret on the D string. The note produced by the harmonic at this fret is a D, so you won't be comparing two notes that are the same, rather two notes a fifth apart. Although you won't hear the pulsing sound created by playing two harmonics together, as in Method 2, it will be very clear if the two notes don't agree.

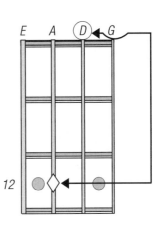

Finally, play the open A and compare it to the 12th-fret harmonic on the E string:

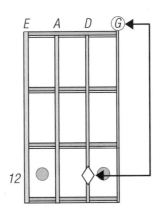

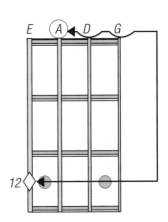

Next play the open D string and compare it to the 12th fret harmonic on the A string:

Any one of these methods is a perfectly acceptable way to tune your bass; it's simply a matter of choosing the one that works best for you.

Personally, I prefer Method 3, but that's just me and my personal opinion! Again, I would recommend having an electronic guitar tuner just to check. This is particularly important for beginners who perhaps haven't had the chance to develop their ears yet.

3 LEARNING THE FRETBOARD

'The majority of musicians can't read music, can't play in different keys on their instruments,
don't know the names of certain sounds and chords and don't know the notes on their guitars.
It's not an insult, it's a fact.' *Jeff Berlin*

Welcome to the most important chapter in this book. I'm serious! Without a good understanding of where the notes are on your bass, you'll be severely limited in how you can progress on the instrument. It stuns me that people who have been playing the bass for a while will still not have bothered to learn their fretboard inside and out – and then they wonder why they're not progressing as quickly as they think they should. Common sense dictates that we should know the fretboard as thoroughly as possible. It's my job to be as helpful as I can, so let's have a look at some of the ways we can make the process easier.

On the next page you'll find a diagram of the bass neck with all the notes written on it. This is for you to refer to when needed. You'll notice that the diagram goes only as far as the 12th fret. This is because after this fret the notes begin to repeat.

Without further ado, let's examine some of the different ways to get those pesky notes off the fretboard and into your head. Use the chart shown on the next page to help you to establish your knowledge of the fretboard.

Method 1

The first method is to start on the low E string and work your way along it, learning the notes as you go. A basic understanding of the alphabet will help a great deal here, since the same rules apply. If you try to remember that there's a sharp/flat (♯/♭) between each note except for between B and C and between E and F, you should find this method a good place to start. Try to say the notes aloud as you go,

as this will help to cement them into your brain. Once you've covered the E string, move on to the other strings.

Method 2

This method is the same as the first in principle, except that it involves learning the notes one fret at a time. Start with the first fret on each string, then the second and so on. You'll find this difficult if you've worked through Method 1, but this highlights a disadvantage of Method 1, which is also shared by Method 2, in that they encourage you to learn the notes parrot-fashion. You'll probably find that you're unable to name any of the notes at random without referring to some of the ones you know before or after them. You might argue that you got there in the end, but you need your knowledge to be more independent. You therefore need to work at randomly naming notes on the neck. Point to any note and name it without having to refer to any others for guidance. Although these two methods have their disadvantages, they're a good place to start.

Method 3

One way that you can expand on the first method and avoid learning by association is to move away from chromatic (ie one fret at a time) movement. This can be done by learning the notes a string at a time, starting on the first fret and then ascending to the third, fifth and so on, missing out every other note. The notes you've missed can be played as you descend the string. Try the exercise below and repeat it on the A, D and G strings.

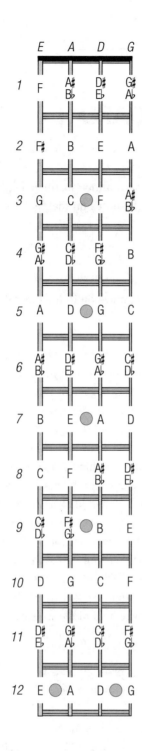

Chart showing the note locations along each string

Method 4

Some people find it easier to learn the notes on the dotted frets first. You'll find that many of these notes are naturals (♮), which makes things a little easier. I recommend learning a few at a time – for example, the notes at the third fret. Again, the trick is to get someone – preferably another bass player/guitarist who knows their fretboard – to test you at random on the notes you've covered. This method is one of the more popular with my students.

Method 5

In this method, you simply learn the notes in the songs that you know. Pick a song that you can play and, using the chart, work out which notes are which. If you pick a simple song, this will obviously be easier. Once you have those notes in mind, get someone to test you at random with the ones that you know. Then move on to another song that you play and work out those notes, too. Eventually, you'll have covered the whole bass.

Method 6

This is probably the most musical way to learn your notes and, at the same time, one of the most frustrating. You might already be aware that there is a lot of repetition on the bass neck. Certain notes occur more than once – for example, the open G is the same as the G at the fifth fret D string, the tenth fret A string and the 15th fret E string. Add that to all the other Gs in various octaves and there are a lot of them about (nine on a 24-fret, four-string bass).

Starting with the low E, try to play all the Es on your bass, in all the different octaves. Then play all the Fs. This can take a while, so it's probably worth taking it a step at a time, depending on what knowledge of the fretboard you already have. I suggest working on one note at a time and moving on only when you're confident that you know it well.

Many people will find that it's through a combination of these methods that they finally get the notes into their head. It really doesn't matter how you learn them, as long as you learn them. Hopefully you'll find that, once you've learnt them, they stick. Have fun!

4 NOTATION AND TABLATURE

'I didn't have a clue about writing or reading music, so I learnt a bit of that, which was brilliant. I also studied different styles and different ways of playing the bass, which was absolutely fantastic to learn.'
Anthony Bishop, bassist with Martin Grech

One of the first questions (or complaints) I hear from students when I bring up the tricky subject of reading music is, 'None of my favourite bass players reads music so why do I need to?' Well, you don't. But even if you don't think you'll ever want or need to read music, it does everyone good to have a basic understanding of the principles involved. These students are usually right about their favourite players – some of the best bass players ever to have walked the Earth don't have a clue how to read music. Among these are Paul McCartney, John Entwistle, Flea, Mark King, Billy Sheehan and many more besides. But equally, some the world's finest bass players can and do read, and it helps them make a living from the thing that they love. In this group we have James Jamerson, Jaco Pastorius, John Patitucci, Jeff Berlin, Victor Wooten, Marcus Miller, Steve Bailey – in fact, pretty much every working professional bassist. Not only will a basic grasp of written music benefit you in every other area of your playing, it will also enable you to communicate with other musicians in a language they'll understand. There's clearly something to be said for it, so hang in there while I try to explain the basics...

Most guitar/bass books available today are notated in a combination of both standard notation and tablature. For those of you who are new to either of these, notation comprises the dots and rhythm parts (the bit we assume is difficult) and tablature is usually written below the

notation (the bit that looks not so difficult). All of the music in this book is notated in both ways. We'll talk more about tab in the second half of this chapter, but for now let's have a look at the fundamentals of notation.

Reading music – or, more specifically, sight-reading music (literally being able to read an unseen piece of music on sight) – is an art in itself and is beyond the scope of this book, although I do take a slightly more in-depth look at it in Chapter 13. I'm not here to turn you into the world's greatest reader, but I am going to try to give you an understanding of how to get started. Hopefully you'll see the ways it can benefit you and you'll be encouraged to pursue it.

Pitch

Music is notated on a set of five horizontal lines called a *stave*, or a *staff*. Notes are placed on the stave either on or between the lines, as shown in the diagram below. At the beginning of the line you'll see what's known as the *bass clef*. A clef is a symbol that tells us what notes the lines and spaces correspond to. For example, the bass clef is occasionally referred to as the *F clef*, as the two dots sit on either side of the line which will hold the note F. From there, it's possible to work out where the rest of the notes will occur. We'll look at those in a moment, but for now here's the bass clef with the open strings of your bass notated on it:

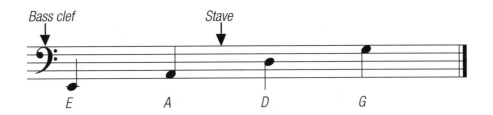

In the next diagram, I've notated all the natural notes from your low E string to the G found at the 12th fret on the G string:

E F G A B C D E F G A B C D E F G

As you can see, sometimes we need to write notes whose pitches are beyond the five lines of the stave. In these instances we have to use *leger lines*. In the above example, the last five notes (C to G) are too high for the stave and are therefore on leger lines. The first note, E, is too low for the stave, so this also sits on a leger line.

Accidentals

You'll notice that so far we haven't covered any sharps or flats – or accidentals, as they're known collectively. That's because these don't occur naturally on the stave; we have to indicate that the note is sharp (♯) or flat (♭) with a symbol. They look like this in use:

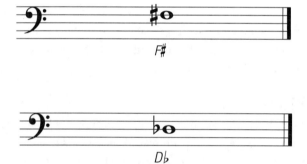

F♯

D♭

A sharp or flat applies to every occurrence of that note for the rest of the bar. If a following note needs to be made into a natural again, it must be indicated by the natural sign (♮). In the next bar, however, the note is automatically natural and you'll need to add another accidental to change it.

As you'll discover, some keys mean that notes will have to be continuously sharpened or flattened. To avoid our music becoming cluttered, we use a system of *key signatures* to indicate that certain notes will be sharp or flat unless indicated otherwise. Key signatures are found at the beginnings of pieces of music and are repeated at the beginning of each new line. Take a look through any music book and you'll see what I mean. In most pieces, you'll see an arrangement of sharps and flats at the start of each line. This tells us what key you're in and which notes are sharp or flat by default. There are 12 major keys and 12 minor, and each is represented by its own key signature. Here are all 12 major keys for you to study:

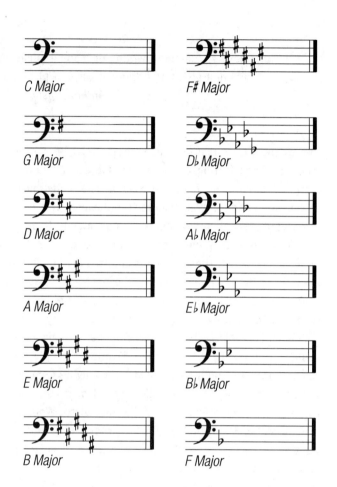

C Major

F♯ Major

G Major

D♭ Major

D Major

A♭ Major

A Major

E♭ Major

E Major

B♭ Major

B Major

F Major

If this is all new to you, I can assure you that things will become clearer as you begin to study your major scales. See Chapter 6 for more on this.

Rhythm

Now that we know about staves, notes and accidentals, we can look at how rhythm is notated. Music is divided up into *bars*, or *measures*, by vertical lines known as *bar lines*. Bar lines break the music up into smaller, easier-to-read chunks.

Before we look specifically at rhythms, however, we must look at *time signatures*. A time signature is a device that tells us how rhythms are arranged. Most Western music is written in 4/4 time, which is by far and away the most common time signature and the only one you'll see in this book. The top number tells us how many beats there are in a bar – in this case, four. The lower number tells us the value of those beats, and in this example the value is a quarter-note, also represented by a four. These values will be explained shortly. You can think of a beat as a foot-tap. Try tapping your foot along to a song on the radio – your foot will be marking the beat. You should be able to count one-two-three-four along to your beats. By doing so, you're marking out 4/4 time.

The rhythmic part of notation comes from the stems and their various groupings that lead upwards or

downwards from the notes. There are several different rhythmic values we can assign to a note – for example, we can make a note last for one beat, two beats, half a beat, a quarter of a beat and so on. The chart below shows the different rhythmic values available and their corresponding rests. You'll notice that I have included both English and American terminology, but I prefer to use the American – it certainly makes more sense!

UK Terminology	US Terminology	Note	Rest	Duration	In Use
Semibreve	Whole note	𝅝	▬	Four beats	𝅝
Minim	Half note	𝅗𝅥	▬	Two beats	𝅗𝅥 𝅗𝅥
Crotchet	Quarter note	♩	𝄽	One beat	♩ ♩ ♩ ♩
Quaver	Eighth note	♪	𝄾	Half beat	♫ ♫ ♫ ♫
Semiquaver	16th note	♬	𝄿	Quarter beat	♬♬ ♬♬ ♬♬ ♬♬

By using combinations of these rhythms, we can notate how we want our music to sound.

In the examples that follow, I will illustrate some of these rhythms. The second part of each example illustrates the use of the rest for the rhythm in question. All of the following examples can be heard on the accompanying CD.

In the first example, there are four quarter notes in a bar – that's one for each beat (or foot-tap):

Below is a bar of half notes. These last for two beats each, so there will be two of them in a bar:

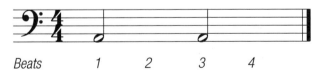
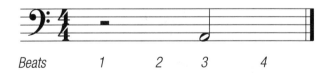

The next example is a bar of eighth notes. Two eighth notes comprise a single beat, so we can play eight of these in a bar:

You'll also notice that, where possible, our eighth notes have been *beamed* together in groups of two. This is for ease of reading, as it makes it clearer for us to see the beat divisions.

Next is a bar of 16th notes. As illustrated in the table on the previous page, there are four 16th notes per beat, so we can have 16 16th notes in a bar.

Obviously, in order to cover the many different rhythmic possibilities, we are going to have to mix and match our rhythms, as shown here:

Tied And Dotted Notes

That's all very well, but what if we want a note to last for a beat and a half? Or for three quarters of a beat? We can use ties or dots to notate those variations. A tie tells you to you hold a note for its duration and the duration of the note that it's tied to.

For example, if you wanted a note to last for a beat and a half, you could write this:

We could also notate the same thing with a dotted note. Adding a dot after a note extends its value by 50 per cent, so a dotted quarter note lasts for a quarter note plus an eighth note, or a beat and a half:

Dotted notes are particularly useful for dividing up 16th-note rhythms, as shown below:

Triplets

The last rhythm to look at is the triplet. A triplet is three evenly played notes in the space of two. There is not a mathematically correct way of notating triplets with the rhythms we have examined so far, so they must be written slightly differently.

In the example below, I've written out a bar of eighth-note triplets:

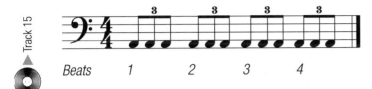

You'll notice the numeral 3 over the groupings in the above examples. This is standard notation and necessary to indicate a triplet.

We can also play quarter-note triplets. Again, the number 3 must be added over the grouping to indicate three notes in the space of two:

Hopefully, the examples I've included here and on the CD will give you a basic understanding of both pitch and rhythm and will help you to understand the mechanics of music notation. Although we've covered the fundamentals here, I would recommend that you do your own investigation – check out the notation for songs that you've learnt and see how they're written. Chapter 15, 'Using Your Ear: Transcribing', looks at the merits of learning to transcribe bass parts for yourself – this will help your reading immensely. I learnt to read by learning how to write down what I heard, which made the process a little more interesting!

Tablature

Tablature, or *tab*, as it's commonly known, is often frowned upon by the 'serious' bass-playing community for being simplistic and having little musical content. It's true that you can get only so much from reading tab, since it doesn't contain any rhythmic information, leaving you having to either guess how to play the notes or listen closely to the track. But tab has its advantages, too. It's great for beginners and works well as a quick-start method for learning your favourite songs. It also shows you where to play the notes on the bass, whereas notation leaves that decision to your best judgement. For example, there are three places on the bass to play the E an octave above the open E string. Where should you play it? It depends on context, of course, but tab will often show you the best place to play it, saving you from having to work it out yourself.

Tab is notated on a stave, which is read from left to right, much like standard notation. However, instead of a stave with five lines, tab uses a four-line stave with each line representing one of the strings on your bass. The top line is the G string, the bottom one the E string and the middle two the A and D strings respectively.

Track 17

Notes are notated according to the fret they occur on. The B found at the seventh fret on the E string would be notated thus:

```
T|--------------------------------------------||
A|--------------------------------------------||
B|--------7-----------------------------------||
```

A G major scale would be written like this:

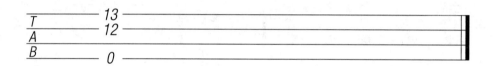

```
T|----------------------------------------------||
A|----------------2---3---5-------2---4---5-----||
B|----3---5---------------------------------------||
```

Any notes played together, such as chords and double stops, would be notated like this:

```
T|--------13------------------------------------||
A|--------12------------------------------------||
B|--------0-------------------------------------||
```

That's about as far as tab-reading goes, but it's lot easier on the eye than standard notation, I think you'll agree!

Remember to bear in mind that tab doesn't give you all the information you need. As I mentioned at the beginning of this section, there's absolutely no rhythmic information contained in tab, so the format does have its limits. However, if you've never read music of any kind, it's the perfect place to start.

5 PRACTISING

'You cannot practise without practice.' Jeff Berlin

For some people, the very thought of practising – even the mention of the word – is enough to send shivers down their spines. But the fact remains that, if you want to be better at something, you need to practise. Would you put faith in a football team that never trained? I don't think so. However, while many bassists think of practice as being pointless hours spent in front of the metronome playing through endless scales and arpeggios, it actually be very different.

Firstly, you don't need to spend five hours a day practising in order to notice an improvement in your playing. In fact, I can assure you that half an hour a day, every day, will yield very surprising results. Secondly, it doesn't have to be boring – honestly! You could even learn to love it, given time. Well, maybe...

But let's go back to that first point. Students often ask me how often they should practise. The answer depends on what you want to get out of your instrument – as I said in the 'Introduction', you get out only what you put in. It stands to reason that, if all you want to do is learn rock songs and play in pubs, you won't require as much practice as the guy who wants to set the world on fire with his mastery of jazz soloing. However, I believe that every bass player should practise every day. As I said, I know for a fact that half an hour a day will change your playing immeasurably – as long as it's practice you're doing...

So what do I mean by that? Well, imagine sitting down to do your half-hour of 'practice'. You run through your favourite licks, play along to your favourite songs and do what you like doing. That isn't practice! That's playing – or noodling – and it's important to differentiate between the two.

Here's the dictionary definition of *practise*: 'Repetition of an activity in order to achieve mastery and fluency.' Doesn't sound much like the half-hour of noodling you just did, does it? Practice, by its very nature, is repeating over and over again something that you cannot do. Playing through your favourite licks isn't practice if you can play them already.

Making A Practice Schedule

So let's think about that half hour of practising. Again, what you practise depends on what you want to do with your instrument. Once you know this, you'll know what to focus on and set your goals accordingly. Goals are important for all musicians, as they give you direction and, when attained, add extra momentum to your enthusiasm. I find that a well-thought-out practice schedule helps both me and my students to achieve what we both want out of our playing. Here are some of the topics that I might practise.

- **Warm-ups** – These are essential for every bass player. It can be very damaging to your hands to play the bass without properly warming up. Tendonitis and repetitive strain injuries (RSI) are just a couple of scary phrases I can shout at you here. Warming up can consist of playing chromatic patterns, a series of scales or just some simple lines at a comfortable tempo. I would recommend doing a minimum of five to ten minutes of warming up before playing.

- **Scale Knowledge** – This is important to any bass player who wants freedom on their instrument. Scales can also replace pattern exercises as more musical warm-ups. I recommend practising for about 10–15 minutes on scales.

- **Sight-Reading** – This is one section that really does depend on what you want from your instrument. For the most part, only bassists who consider playing for a living will feel that they need this skill. Nevertheless, I consider it very important for all players.

- **Technique** – Having problems with your slap technique? Your string crossing or your raking? Practice will cure all of this, and it's important to devote time to honing your technique.

- **Tunes** – The more songs you know, the easier you'll find life as a bass player. Whether it's learning the new song by your favourite band or finding your way through a tricky jazz chart, this is one of the most important aspects of practice.

- **Difficult Licks** – I also find it useful to keep a small list of licks that I struggle with. A little work on them every day ensures that I progress with them.

Learning It Twice

Have you ever tried learning something new only to find that your hands can't keep up with your brain or vice versa? I have, and I've come to the conclusion that you need to learn new material twice: first in your head and then in your hands.

When approaching a new lick try this: look through the music first without touching your bass. Check out notes and position shifts, anything that may present a problem. Now grab your bass and play through it slowly. Give your fingers a chance to learn where they need to go. Go over tricky passages bit by bit, making sure that you understand what's going on.

Now work with your new music and practise it. Play it a little quicker if you can. Build on what you've learnt so far, concentrating on the weaker aspects and bringing them up to speed. This approach is infinitely better than rushing in and trying to play an awkward piece at speed straight away.

Your Surroundings

You need to be comfortable when you practise. By 'comfortable' I mean sat in a chair that supports your back and in quiet, pleasant surroundings. Finding a good chair to sit in is important, as playing the bass tends to encourage us to hunch. Find a chair that supports your lower back and resist the temptation to hunch over, staring at the fretboard. Most basses these days have side position markers on the frets, so there should be no excuse for hunchback impressions!

Very few bass players practise standing up. Maybe it's because we're incredibly lazy, I don't know. Whatever the explanation, practising when you're sitting down encourages you to play in a certain way. The angles of your arms are different then, which in turn could change your approach to some techniques. (See Chapter 11, 'Slap Bass', for more on this). Because of this, I always recommend setting your strap height so that, when you stand up to play, the bass remains where it would be when you're sitting – roughly,

at least. If you don't do this, you'll have to adjust to a different playing position each time you stand up/sit down.

Almost as important is to try to find a time in the day when you're least likely to be disturbed – you're not going to get anything constructive done with people walking in and out of the room and talking to you, so try to find a quiet practice area. I also find it very useful to be organised. Have everything you need with you: music paper, books, pens, leads and so on should all be within easy reach.

Practising with either a metronome or a drum machine is essential. I was once taught a very useful practising trick with a metronome. Set your tempo, but imagine that the click is the offbeat. Your tempo will look like this:

one (click) two (click) three (click) four (click)...

The benefit of this system is that, because you're not actually playing on the click, it checks you after you've played. Learning to work with a metronome encourages good time-keeping.

Even if you're still not particularly enamoured with practising, you will notice that, aside from the obvious benefit of improving on the bass, it will help your creativity. As part of my practice regime, I play grooves along with a beat. I try to alternate my rhythms so that one day I'm playing funk, whereas another day I might be playing reggae, and so on. Mostly I'll come up with either a line, a fill or a chord that interests me, and that I probably would never have thought of ordinarily.

Now, here's the key to this: if you come with a new idea, write it down! I keep a note pad handy and jot down everything – solo ideas, chord voicings, fills, the lot. This means that I have a note pad full of ideas that I can continue practising, add to my repertoire or develop as I see fit.

When I learn something – be it a new lick or bass line that I particularly like – I try to play it in every key. Doing so encourages me to explore some of the less pleasant keys to play in. I mean, what bass player feels comfortable in G♭? Well, ideally you should feel comfortable in any key, and by practising your licks in all 12, you can be. Pick a bass line you like. Set a metronome going and play the line through in its home key. After playing it two or three times, move to a new key and practise it there. You can move to different keys in various ways – by going up or down a fret chromatically or by following a set pattern of keys. I prefer to follow a pattern of keys called the *circle of fifths* (see Chapter 6). I start my line in C, play it through a few times, then do it in G, then D, and so on. This means that I get around the entire instrument – even the dusty end!

6 MAJOR SCALES

'If you're playing in an improvised setting, harmonic knowledge is necessary.' *Laurence Cottle*

Welcome to the first of two chapters on everyone's least-favourite subject: scales. Now, I'm not going to try to convince you that scales are particularly enjoyable to play, because they're not, but if you want to develop your bass playing, you're going to need them, and what's more, you're going to have to practise them. A lot. Well, quite a bit, anyway. But I'm hoping that when you know just a little more about them – and you begin to see how they are going to help you become a better player and musician – it will make all that hard work and practice a little easier to bear.

At the most basic level, scales are the raw material of music – the bricks we build our musical houses out of, if you like. For a bass player, and indeed any musician (except drummers, maybe!), scales serve many useful purposes, and you'll benefit from having at least some knowledge of them.

I'm often asked, and I often used to wonder myself, what are scales actually for? There are several answers: they will help free your creativity on the bass and enable you to play in all keys; they will enable you to solo convincingly; they make good warm-up exercises; they're great for left- and right-hand development and dexterity. I could go on, but suffice to say they're basically pretty useful.

As I've already mentioned, to get the most out of scales you'll need to practise them quite religiously. I strongly recommend working them into your daily practice routine, if you have one. (If you haven't go back and read Chapter 5 again!) Spending 10–15 minutes a day working methodically with your scales will improve your playing in many directions at once. You'll have to trust me on this for the time being.

Scale Types

There are two main types of scale: major and minor. What follows is a fairly in-depth look at major scales (minor scales are covered in the next chapter) and what I think

is the best way to go about learning them. Fear not, I will attempt to take you through them a step at a time, demystifying them and explaining carefully as I go.

The information presented here is designed to be cumulative – by working through this chapter in order you'll be gradually adding to your knowledge in small chunks, and by the end you should be well equipped to start on the second chapter. I strongly recommend that you take this information at a pace you're comfortable with and learn it thoroughly. However, I appreciate that much of what you do with this information will depend on what you want from your bass, so some of you might find that some of the exercises offer a bit more than you want – or indeed need – to know.

Major Exercise

With the following exercises, I'm going to assume that you know the fretboard of your bass pretty well – you won't be able to find your way around these scales properly without knowing where all the notes are. As discussed in Chapter 3, good fretboard knowledge is fundamental to any bass player, so if you have any doubt about what some of those frets are for, I suggest that you do a little homework! It's also worth mentioning that you should familiarise yourself with the sound of the major scale – it should be familiar to you; it's basically the same as that old tune 'Doh-Ray-Me'. Keep your ears open when you're playing, don't shut off and don't just play through them mindlessly – listen to what you're doing.

It's also useful to try singing the scale as you play it. Don't be shy! It's very useful for a bass player to develop his/her ear, and singing along helps! See Chapter 14 for more on developing your ear.

Okay, pep-talk over. Let's start at the very beginning and look at how to play a basic major scale. Here's the fingering for a C major scale starting from the C at the third fret on the A string:

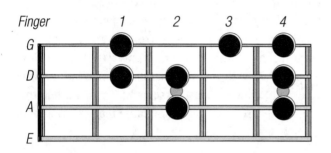

Exercise 1

In between the staves I've written the left-hand fingering that I would suggest using. This system is known as the 'finger per fret' system and is explained in more detail in Chapter 8. It's fairly obvious when you look at what we are playing. A major scale in this position covers four frets and we have four fingers on our left hand – makes sense to use them all, doesn't it? This is illustrated below:

Finger   1   2   3   4

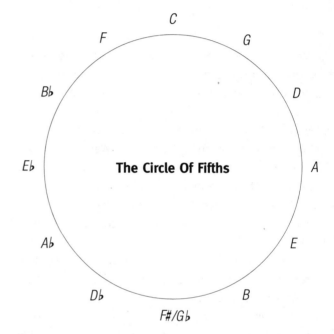

The Circle Of Fifths

Using this system will greatly help the dexterity of your left hand and encourage you to use all of your fingers.

It stands to reason that, by moving this shape around, you could play a major scale in any key you liked simply by moving the whole thing to a different fret. Go ahead and try it: move this pattern up so that your second finger is on the eighth fret, an F. Because the intervals (ie the distances between the notes) haven't changed, the sound is almost the same; you're simply playing it in a new key. (You can hear me play an F major scale on the CD.) Now, when someone asks you to play any of the 12 major scales, you have my permission to get smug!

I'm a great advocate of playing through all of your major scales at least a couple of times a week. It doesn't take long and is good for your hands, your ears and definitely for your brain. I practise my scales according to a sequence called the *circle of fifths*. This is simply a representation of all 12 keys, each one a fifth up from the last. It looks like this:

A complete explanation of the circle of fifths at this point would involve many pages of very boring music theory, and at this point I don't really want to scare you off! For the moment, it's enough simply to absorb the basics – leave the tricky stuff until later. Any good music dictionary or theory book will give you a complete grounding in it if you're interested, however.

All of this brings us to our first exercise in this chapter. Set a metronome going at a nice easy tempo – somewhere around 80 beats per minute (bpm) should be about right – and play though your C major scale. Stick to crotchets (quarter notes) at this point, as there isn't much to be gained by ripping through these at 1,000 miles per hour!

Next, move on to the G major scale, then the D, and so on. Try not to break your flow between scales – you have time to be thinking ahead and looking to where you'll need to move as you play. The first three keys – C, G, and D – are performed on the CD.

Here's the beginning of the exercise:

Exercise 2

etc...

Hopefully that made at least some sense! Make sure that you can play and understand what we've covered so far before moving on. At this point you don't need to know what notes are in each scale and why – we'll get to that shortly. This exercise should serve to get you comfortable playing the major scale in different places on the bass, and it also makes a good warm-up exercise!

Content Over Patterns

You'd be forgiven for thinking that the obvious thing to do next would be to steam ahead and learn two-octave major scales. Well, here's a surprise: that's not what we're going

to do – at least not yet. I believe that doing this would result in simply learning another pattern and not addressing the notes themselves – not learning much actual content. Instead, I'm going to suggest what I believe is a much more musical path. You might have to work a little harder, but I think you'll find that the benefits are significantly greater than they would be if I simply gave you some patterns and showed you how to shift them around. No, I believe the best way forward is to go back now and learn the notes involved in a one-octave scale and then apply that knowledge to playing two octave scales and more. I hope I'm not scaring you too much!

Let's go back to that C major scale we started with. You'll notice that it's made up purely of natural notes – no sharps or flats. In fact, it's the only major scale that is, which makes it the perfect place to start. Here are the notes of the C major scale:

Armed with this piece of knowledge, it stands to reason that we could pick any C on the bass and play the scale from there – it's just all the natural notes from that point, right? Well, let's try it! Start on the same C as before and play through all the natural notes on the same string until you get back to C again. If you did it correctly, you'll have played this:

C D E F G A B C

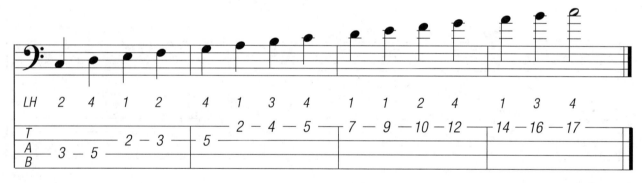

Exercise 3

By knowing the content of the scale rather than just a pattern, which is of limited real use, we can put our knowledge to work in new ways. If I'm doing my job properly here, playing a two-octave major scale shouldn't sound quite so bad now...

Well, we're all friends here, so let's give it a try. Start on the C and then play up through the natural notes to the next C, then to the next one. You'll undoubtedly notice that

at some point you're going to have to move to another string. But where? There are many points at which you could jump, and no right or wrong ones. The benefit of what you've just learned is that, by knowing the notes in the scale, you can play through it in many ways – a different way each time, if you wish. This helps you to learn the scale over the whole fretboard and is the benefit of learning scales as content rather than as patterns.

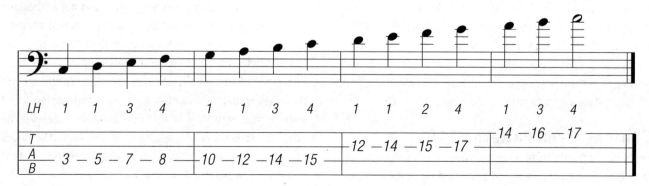

Exercise 4a

I did promise to be helpful, however, so here's another way that you could have played your two-octave C major scale:

Exercise 4b

If this is all new to you, then I would suggest you take it all nice and slow and just practise a little every day. For the first few days, you'll probably find yourself sticking to the fingerings I suggested above, but I'm betting that after a while you'll start to notice different ones, too. This is your knowledge leading you, rather than the other way around.

The Next Step

Once you're completely happy with your first scale, it's time to learn another one. Don't forget that there are 12 keys to learn in all! Fortunately, if you learn all of your scales in the order shown by the circle of fifths, you'll be building on what you've learnt previously, and in small, manageable steps.

Consulting the circle of fifths will reveal that the next scale is G major. To start with, let's play a one-octave G major scale starting on the G located at the third fret on the E string. Remember that our one-octave pattern from earlier is moveable along the fretboard, so all the intervals and fingering will remain the same. Here's how it looks on paper:

◀ Track 23

Assuming that you know the fretboard, you'll have noticed that this scale differs very little (by only one note) to the C major scale. In fact, you should notice that it's almost identical. This is because, by moving sequentially around the circle of fifths in this manner, each scale will contain only one different note from the last. Cool, huh? If you don't believe me, take a pen and paper and write the notes down for yourself. You'll see this:

G A B C D E F♯ G

The G major scale is different from the C major by just one note – our F has become an F♯.

Now have a go at playing through a G major scale on just the E string, armed with this new knowledge. The illustration below shows what you'll have hopefully ended up playing:

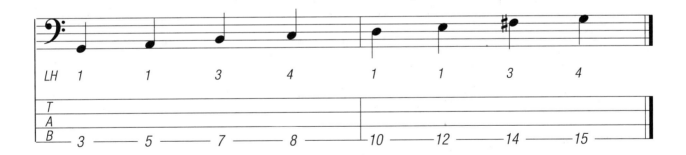

Now let's try a two-octave G major scale. As with the C major scale, there are many different ways of playing this and you should avoid sticking to any particular one – again,

thorough fretboard knowledge will enable you to find many different possibilities. For your convenience, I've illustrated a couple of ways in which you can do it:

Exercise 5

There are ten more major scales for you to learn. Be careful not to bite off more than you can chew and move on to the next scale only when you're happy with the last one. Learning your scales in this way is much more musical and really tests your knowledge of the fretboard. With scales, as with any other aspect of playing the bass, if you find it difficult I would suggest that you try to see it as a challenge rather than an obstacle and push past it. If you find something difficult, that usually means that it's worth doing!

Once you know your scales well enough to play two-octave scales in myriad positions all over the bass, you can progress to the next level. We'll now play a C major scale from the lowest note on the bass.

Knowing our scales as we do will tell us that the lowest note we have available in the key of C is an E (I'm assuming that you're playing on a standard four-string bass here). We're going to play four bars ascending and then four bars descending:

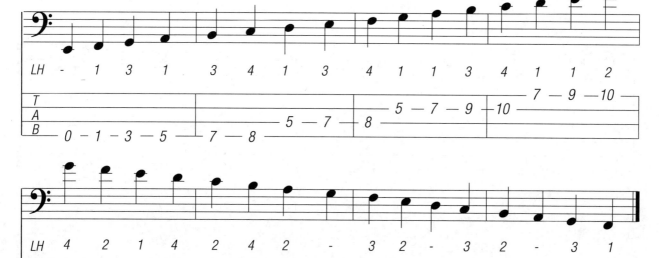

You'll notice that the fingering that I've suggested in the tab is only one of many possible ways to play through this exercise. There are too many different ways to list, but here's another possibility for you to consider:

Exercise 6

Try to use a different fingering when descending, as in the above exercises.

The final exercise in this chapter (Exercise 8) is the one I use both to warm up with and to practise my scales and fretboard knowledge – effectively killing three birds with one stone! As illustrated above, I play through the exercise in C, then I go around the circle of fifths, playing through the other 11 keys – it doesn't take as long as you think!

Nevertheless, I don't recommend attempting this until you know each scale well enough to play one- and two-octave versions all over the bass. Set your metronome at a comfortable tempo (I recommend 80 beats per minute) for this exercise, since to start with you'll probably need to give yourself time to think about what you're doing. As I've already said, practising this every day will yield surprising results and will benefit your playing in many ways.

C major

Track 26

Exercise 7

G major

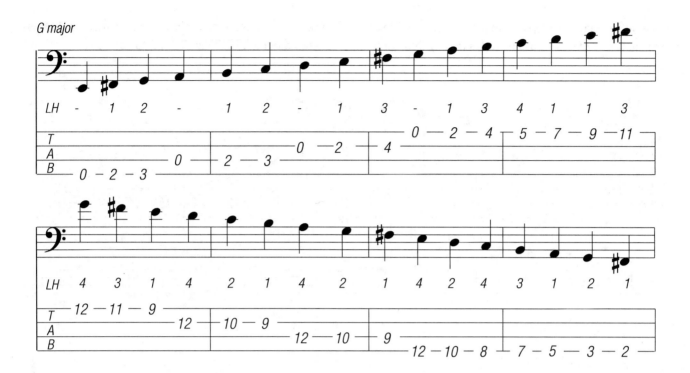

D major

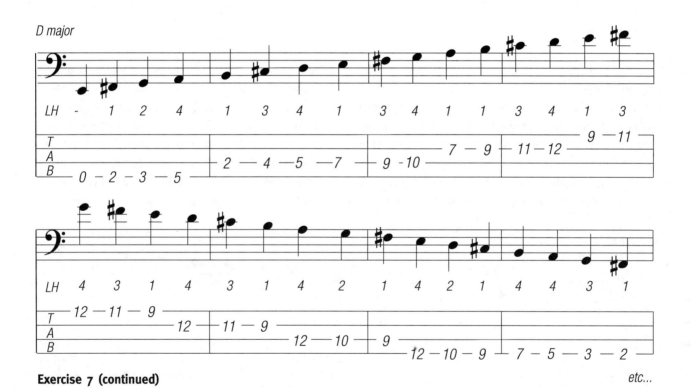

Exercise 7 (continued) *etc...*

Once you're comfortable with the exercise, try the following:

- Go around the circle of fifths backwards. You'll actually be moving around it in fourths, which is also very useful for those of you who like to play jazz;

- Devise new orders in which to practise the keys – for example, play every other key: C, D, E, F♯, A♭, B♭, then F, G, A, B, D♭, E♭;

- If you get stuck in a rut and you find yourself constantly sticking to the same old patterns and going over them over and over again, try playing all the way up the scale on the E string and back down on the A string.

- Try playing as much as you can in the first five frets before ascending through the rest of the scale on the G string. Descend using a different route.

7 MINOR SCALES

'Harmony and theory can be helpful if you're thinking of writing tunes.' *Laurence Cottle*

Unfortunately, minor scales are slightly more complicated than their major cousins. This is mainly because there are no less than three different types of minor scale, and no one ever seems completely sure which one to use. These three types are the *natural minor*, the *harmonic minor* and the *melodic minor*. Now for some good news: straight away we are going to dispense with one of these, the melodic minor, as it's not a scale with which you as a bassist need to be immediately familiar. Here's another piece of good news: if you have successfully worked through the previous chapter on major scales, you're going to find this chapter pretty easy, since we're going to be building on what knowledge of scales you've already acquired – all will become clear soon, I promise. Hopefully I'm still doing my job of making things easier to understand, and by the time you've finished this chapter you'll know exactly what a minor scale is and how to play one.

The Natural Minor Scale

We're going to start with the natural minor scale. Now, as I mentioned above, if you've worked through the previous chapter on major scales, you won't find these too hard.

'Why's that?' I hear you ask. The answer is that you already know them. Suspend your disbelief for a moment so that I can attempt to explain: every natural minor scale is, in fact, one of the major scales you've learnt already, just starting from a different note – in musical terms, we say that they are related. Consider the following fretboard diagram of a natural minor scale:

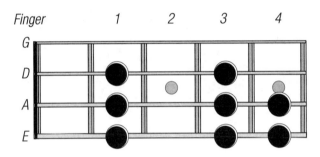

Let's play through this scale from the A on your E string, as in Exercise 1 below. You'll immediately hear that our A minor scale doesn't sound quite as jolly as the good old major scale. In fact, at a very basic level you can think of major scales as sounding 'happy' and minor ones as 'sad.'

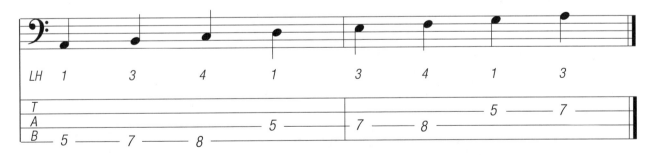

Exercise 1

Now let's examine the notes you've just played. If you write down each note in the A minor scale, you'll get this: A, B, C, D, E, F, G, A.

I'm hoping that alarm bells are now ringing in your head and that you have spotted that this scale doesn't

contain any sharps or flats. This being the case, you might also have noticed that it contains the same notes as the C major scale – but they're now in a different order. This is because the A minor scale is the *relative minor* of the C major scale.

Relative Minors

Each major scale has a relative minor scale which contains exactly the same notes. To find a major scale's corresponding relative minor scale, you simply count up through the degrees of the major scale to the sixth degree – the relative minor scale is built on the sixth degree of the major scale.

$$C\ D\ E\ F\ G\ \textcircled{A}\ B\ C$$
$$1\ 2\ 3\ 4\ 5\ \textcircled{6}\ 7\ 8$$

This is true of every major scale, so you'll now be able to go through each of your major scales and find their relative minors. Here, though, I've done it for you:

Major Scale	Relative Minor Scale
C	Am
G	Em
D	Bm
A	F#m
E	C#m
B	G#m
F#/Gb	D#/Ebm
Db	Bbm
Ab	Fm
Eb	Cm
Bb	Gm
F	Dm

If you already know some of what I am telling you here, you'd be forgiven for thinking that I'm going to start talking about modes. I'm afraid not. Modes are a difficult subject and are shrouded in mystery – actually, that's something of an exaggeration, but they are certainly beyond the scope of this book. Very briefly (to satisfy curiosity), a mode is simply a major scale played through from a different starting note. In effect, the A natural minor scale is a mode of C major. Each major scale has seven modes. For the time being, at least, that's about as much as you need to know.

As I mentioned in the previous chapter, it's important to learn the content of the scale rather than simply learn a load of patterns, so for the rest of the exercises I'm going to make the following two, rather bold, assumptions:

* That you know your fretboard;
* That you know the note content of at least some, if not all, of your major scales.

With these assumptions in mind, let's think about how we might play an A minor scale on just one string. As I stated above, if you know your fretboard, this won't present a problem to you. A quick recap on what we've covered so far in this chapter will tell you that A minor is related to C major and therefore contains the same notes – no sharps or flats. Common sense dictates that playing an A minor scale from A will include only the natural notes. So without further ado, let's give it a try:

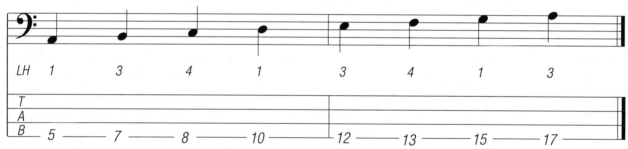

Exercise 2

Hopefully you've played the same as the exercise above.

Now, by combining our knowledge of the scale with our knowledge of the fretboard, we should be able to play a two-octave A minor scale. As in the previous chapter, there are numerous different fingerings for doing this, and the following exercise is just one of them:

Exercise 3

Here's another way you could have played it, this time starting from the open A string:

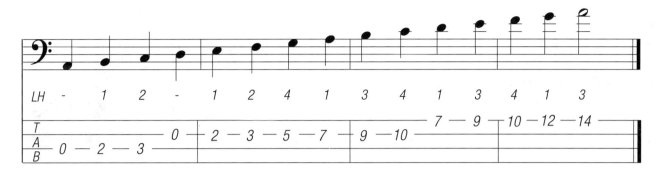

Exercise 4

As with the major scales, you should explore the different ways of playing this scale. To begin with you may find that you stick to the two patterns I've illustrated here, which is fine, but as you become familiar with the sound and notes of the scale you're bound to find new ways to play it. Try to cover as much of the instrument as you can when learning a scale – scales are most useful when you can play them anywhere on the instrument.

If you find an area of the bass you're not confident with – the higher register, for example – make a point of learning what notes live up there and practising your scales there as well.

At this point I suggest that you make sure you've fully understood the concepts presented thus far. If you find yourself struggling with these exercises I would suggest

that you stop here and spend some time working on your fretboard knowledge and what we've looked at so far in this chapter.

The next step is to start learning the other minor scales. If you know your major scales, this should be fairly straightforward since you will in effect be playing exactly the same notes as the corresponding relative major. Try to memorise which major and minor scales relate to each other – it will make things easier. I recommend consulting the chart on the previous page and working through it methodically – A minor, E minor, and so on. Be sure to take the rest of the minor scales one at a time and be careful not to bite off more than you can chew. For reference, here's the next scale in the sequence, E minor, shown here in a two-octave version:

Track 29

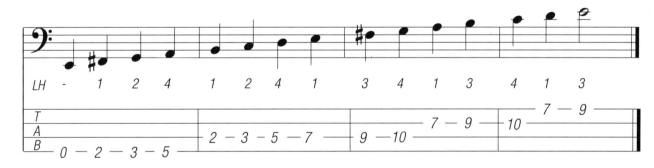

Exercise 5

Looking at the scale and the chart will reveal that the E minor scale is related to the G major scale and therefore contains the same notes – all naturals except the F, which has become an F♯:

E F♯ G A B C D E

You should remember the monster final exercise from the chapter on major scales. You'll recall that we played each of the 12 scales for eight bars, ascending and descending, from the lowest available note. If we were to do the same with the natural minor scales, we would be playing exactly the same exercise, so by practising your major scales in this way you're also practising your minors. The important thing is to remember which major scale relates to which minor. Once you've completed this stage you can move on to the next section, harmonic minor scales. This is where things get a little trickier...

Harmonic Minor Scales

Before you start on harmonic minor scales, I strongly recommend that you have a good understanding of what we've covered so far on natural minors. By doing so you'll save yourself a lot of work, since you're going to build on your knowledge of the natural minors.

Harmonic minor scales differ from natural minor scales by just one note, the seventh degree of the scale, or the *leading note*, as it's known. In the harmonic minor scale the seventh degree is sharpened – so, in the example of the A minor scale, the G is sharpened, becoming a G♯. To the right is the fingerboard pattern for an A harmonic minor scale:

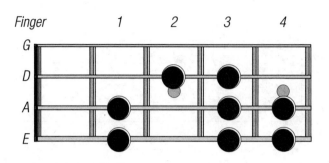

Play through the scale shown in Exercise 6 below. You'll immediately hear that it has a distinctly different sound to the natural minor scale. It's obviously still a minor scale, but it has a more 'Spanish' flavour to it, for want of a better word!

Track 30

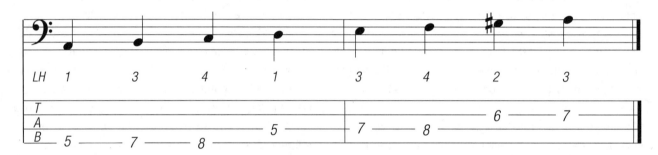

Exercise 6

By knowing the theory behind this scale – that it's the same as the natural minor but with a sharpened leading note – we should be able to adapt our natural minors to harmonic minors by simply altering that one note. Let's put that theory into practice and play an A harmonic minor scale on just the E string:

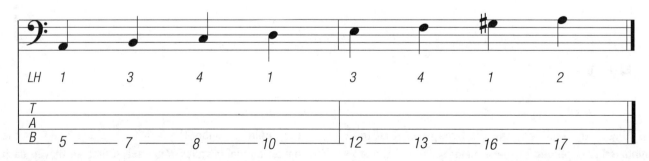

Exercise 7

Again, using what we've learned so far, we can adapt a two-octave A natural minor scale into an A minor harmonic scale:

▲ Track 31

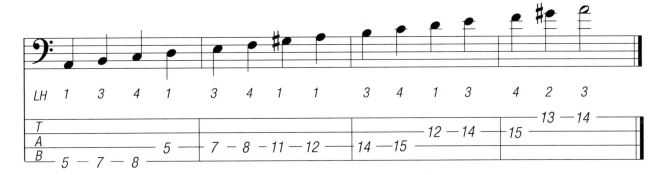

Exercise 8a

Here's an alternative fingering:

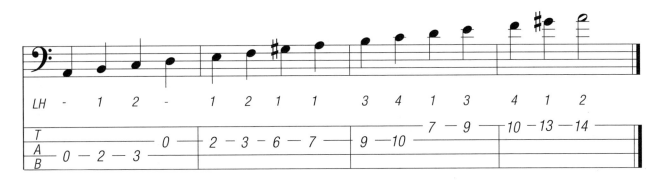

Exercise 8b

You'll notice that the interval between the F and G♯ presents some fingering problems in that it's a larger interval than you would expect to find in a major or minor scale. Make sure that, when playing through any of the previous three exercises, you follow the fingering that I have notated between the staves.

There's little else I need to say about harmonic minors at this point. Now it's simply down to you to learn the other 11! Once you have learnt these thoroughly, make sure you practise them from the lowest available scale tone on your bass in all keys, as in the last exercise of the previous chapter (Exercise 7). Once you have all this knowledge under your belt, you'll be able to play through all your major and minor scales in two exercises. Not only that, but the nature of how you've learnt them means that you should be continuously finding new ways to play them using different areas of the fingerboard.

Overview

With this chapter and the previous one I have attempted to present scales in a way that most people with a basic knowledge of the bass can understand. That said, the beginners among you might find some of this information

a little daunting despite my best efforts to explain it simply! If that's the case, learning a little about music theory should help. There are many textbooks on music theory available. In addition to this, I strongly recommend that everyone study this information in the order it is presented.

The idea is for the concepts you've learnt here to be cumulative – I've tried to base each section on what you've learnt previously. It makes sense to start off with your major scales one at a time, building on them so that you can play them all over the bass. By doing this you free yourself from being restricted to playing within a pattern that you've memorised. You'll need to bear in mind that it will take time to get to this stage, but I believe that you'll be learning the material in the most effective way. By building on your knowledge of major scales, you've learnt that natural minor scales are directly related to the major scales that we have already learnt and that we simply need to remember which ones relate to which. Finally, you can build on all of this to arrive at harmonic minor scales, which differ from the natural minors by just one sharpened note.

There's a lot of information contained in these chapters. It's vital that you take these exercises at a pace that you can deal with and not feel obligated to move through them too quickly. I recommend that you practise scales for 15 minutes a day in your normal practice routine. If you feel like doing more, then by all means do so, but remember what I said in the Introduction about setting yourself reasonable goals. Good luck with them, and trust me – you'll be glad you made the effort!

8 THE LEFT HAND

'I practise scales and exercises I've worked out over the years to help with my
right- and left-hand co-ordination.' *Laurence Cottle*

You might be wondering what you'll find in a chapter focusing on the left hand. Surely, we should be focusing on the right hand, looking at slap techniques and how to get those lightning-fast fingerstyle runs? All in good time. Many people neglect their left hands, not realising that they need just as much attention with regards to technique as their right. Every player has four fingers on their left hand, but many don't utilise the full potential of them. It's all too common for bassists to neglect the third or fourth fingers, whereas if they were to put them to use they would find many bass lines and chord shapes a lot easier. Being able to play fast and, more importantly, accurately doesn't just involve the right hand; you will need to develop your left hand as well and strengthen up those weaker fingers. That's what this chapter is all about.

Fretboard Accuracy

Firstly, you need to make sure that you're playing on the correct part of the fret. You'd be forgiven for thinking that, because your bass has frets, you can play anywhere between the frets and it will sound okay. Technically that's true, but by ignoring accurate placement you will create problems in your playing that will be trickier to solve later on, when you've got used to them.

Try playing a G on your E string with your finger in the centre of the fret. You should find that it sounds pretty good. Now move your finger closer to either one of the frets. You'll hear that you're starting to get some fairly nasty fret buzz. We want to keep noises like that out of our bass playing, so for all of these exercises and, indeed, for everything else you play, try to keep to the centre of the fret.

Chromatic Exercises

You may have seen some of the following exercises before and are now groaning, and I guess they are pretty boring, but while they might sound bad and have little actual musical content, they do serve one useful purpose, and that is to get your fingers working in all sorts of unusual ways. In each of these exercises, we'll utilise the finger-per-fret method. Each exercise is based on four chromatic frets (that's four frets next to each other), and since we have four fingers on our left hands it makes sense to use them all. As the exercises have little musical relevance, I've notated them in tab only. All of these exercises are to be played slowly – accuracy and tone are the important points here and there's little to be gained from playing them too quickly.

In Exercise 1 below we're going to use the first four frets on each string in ascending, then descending, order. Remember to keep each finger in the centre of the fret:

▲ Track 34

Exercise 1

When ascending, try to keep each finger in place while you play the next. If you have small hands, or find that they aren't sufficiently flexible to stretch like this, try moving the exercise to a higher fret where the spacing is narrower – the fifth fret is a good place. When you become happy in this position, see if you can move back to the first fret.

Exercise 2 below is basically the same, except that we're going to apply a new rule: when you run out of fingers, move up one fret. Confused? Me too, but a quick look at the tab should clear things up:

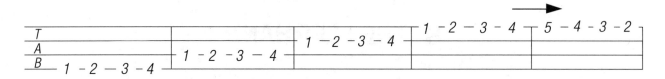

Exercise 2

Exercise 3 goes by many different names, but I like to call it the Snake. You'll see why when you play it:

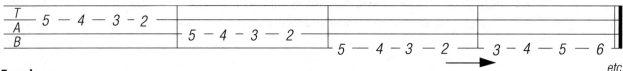

Exercise 3

So far, we've used our fingers only in ascending and descending order: 1, 2, 3, 4 and 4, 3, 2, 1. There are literally hundreds of different combinations of patterns for your fingers to explore and I'll leave it up to you to discover all of the various possibilities.

For now, let's look at three different fingerings, each one using a different finger to lead with. This exercise is fingered 3, 4, 2, 1:

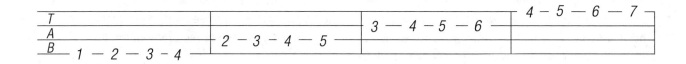

Exercise 4

Now let's try 2, 1, 3, 4:

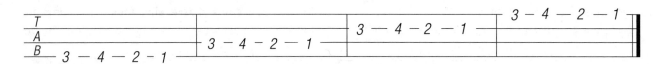

Exercise 5

And finally 1, 4, 3, 2:

```
T
A
B  1 — 4 — 3 - 2 | 1 - 4 - 3 - 2 | 1 — 4 - 3 — 2 | 1 - 4 — 3 — 2 ‖
```

Exercise 6

As I said, there are many different combinations and I'm sure that you'll be able to work out plenty more for yourself. If you find one that's particularly difficult, add it immediately to your practice routine. If you can't do it, you need to practise it, since whatever fingers are holding you back are clearly too weak and need strengthening.

But why stick to only one string at a time? This is where chromatic exercises get both very nasty and extremely good for your hands at the same time.

In the following exercise (Exercise 7), we will take a pattern (1, 2, 4, 3) but move every second-finger note to a different string, like this:

Exercise 7

A little more difficult, I think you'll agree! Again, there a hundreds of different fingering combinations. Let's look at

a couple of other tricky ones; take a look at Exercise 8, tabbed out below.

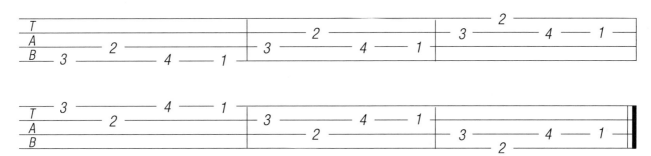

Exercise 8

And Exercise 9:

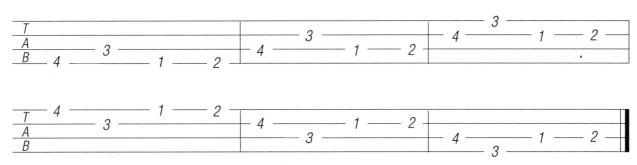

Exercise 9

Of course, you could also move more than one finger at a time. Try this exercise:

```
T |------------------------------------|----------------------------------|------------------2----------4---|
A |---------2---------------------4--|-1------2--------3------------4--|-1--------------3----------------|
B |-1---------------3-------------------|--------------------3--------------|----------------------------------|
```

```
T |--1------------3-----------------|----------------------------------|--------------------------------||
A |---------2---------------4------|-1------------3------------------|-1--------------3--------------||
B |----------------------------------|--------2------------4--------|-----------2------------4-----||
```

Exercise 10

You'll really be feeling the strain in exercises like these, so remember to take it easy and be careful not to hurt your hands. As you're stretching your hands in ways that we were probably never intended to be stretched, it's bound to cause a little discomfort to start with. If it hurts, stop and take a rest. Don't overdo it – you'll be no use to anyone if your hand seizes up!

These exercises are designed for one thing only, and that is to increase your finger dexterity and strength. Building up these aspects of your left hand will help you in many ways, whatever style of bass you play. Hopefully, through practising these on a daily basis, you'll strengthen up those weaker fingers. They make pretty good warm-up exercises and, as I mentioned in Chapter 5, it's important to warm up before doing any serious playing. Ten minutes' practice with some of these exercises every day should see you well on your way to having a strong left hand that isn't going to let you down on those lightning-fast runs or slapped arpeggios!

9 PHRASING TECHNIQUES

'I'm more interested in talking about how to phrase a melody and create a solo that goes someplace.' Stu Hamm

Now that you've looked at the various ways in which you can strengthen and develop your left-hand fingers, it's time to look at the some of the phrasing techniques available. The left hand is very important for phrasing, which forms a large part of that indefinable character which gives each player his own unique sound. The way in which you phrase something defines who you are as a player, and the more phrasing choices you have, the smoother and more fluid your playing will be.

The left hand is responsible for a whole host of phrasing techniques, from slurs (hammer-ons and pull-offs) to string bending and all the different varieties of vibrato. The good thing about all of the phrasing tools that we will look at over the next few pages is that they can be applied to any style of music. Once you've mastered them, you'll use them every day in your playing – in fact, it's pretty likely that you already do. In this chapter we will examine each technique in turn. You'll also be able to hear examples of them on the accompanying CD.

Slurs: Hammer-Ons And Pull-Offs

These two strange-sounding customers are types of slurs. A slur is defined as 'a curved line written over two notes indicating that they are to be played legato or in the same stroke'. Here's an example of both a hammer-on and a pull-off, both of which are described in detail below.

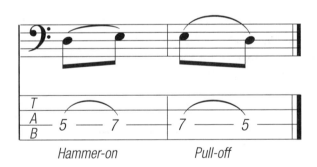

Hammer-on   Pull-off

The Hammer-On

This is the first and most obvious phrasing tool, and it's also one of the most useful. With a hammer-on, a note is played and then another left-hand finger 'hammers' on another note further up on the same string. Using this technique you can play two or more notes after plucking the string only once.

Let's try the example above. Play the D at the fifth fret of your A string – use the first finger of your left hand to fret the note. Once you've played the note, bring your third or fourth finger of the left hand down onto the E at the seventh fret. You'll need to do this quite firmly in order to produce a strong, clear note, and you should aim for both notes to be pretty much the same volume.

Since you have four left-hand fingers, you can probably see that it's possible to hammer on two or three notes in succession. You can hear the example I have just described on the CD – I have played it a few times, first slowly, then a little quicker. Try to mimic the sound you hear on the CD.

▲ Track 37

The Pull-Off

The pull-off is basically a backwards hammer-on. To play a pull-off, place your left-hand first finger on the D at the fifth fret of the A string. Place the third or fourth finger on the E at the seventh fret. Play the string – this will sound the note E. As the note is still ringing, remove your fourth finger from the string. This will allow the fretted D to sound. You will find that you need to pull at the string with your finger slightly as you lift it – this will create movement in the string and allow the note to sound. Again, try to aim for the same volume with both notes. As with hammer-ons, it is possible to play multiple pull-offs using more of your left-hand fingers.

While it's important to try to play both notes of each example at the same volume, you'll also notice a difference in attack. The first one will have a slightly sharper attack because it has been plucked, while the second will sound different because you've slurred it. Hammer-ons and pull-offs enable you to play in a more fluid, legato manner, which can only be a good thing. Let's take a look at some of the other slurring options.

Slides

Slides also come under the umbrella of slurs. You may sometimes see a slanted line connecting two notes as well as the curved slur line over them. This means that you slide from one note to the next, plucking only the first note. On the CD you can hear the earlier hammer-on and pull-off examples played as slides.

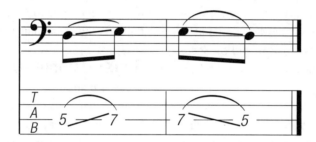

▲ Track 39

Trills

A trill is a combination of hammer-ons and pull-offs played in rapid succession. As in the other examples, only the first note is struck; the rest of the notes are created by hammering on and pulling off. A trill is indicated by the letters *tr* over a note, followed by a wavy line. A trill lasts for the duration of the note over which it's written. You can hear an example of a trill on the CD.

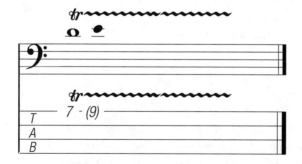

▲ Track 40

Vibrato

Vibrato is a rapid variation in the pitch of a note, played by shaking the fretting finger vertically or horizontally. Vibrato is notated by a wavy line over the note. The method of vibrato most commonly used by guitarists and bassists is to shake the string vertically. To do this, play a note, then move the string up and down slightly with your left-hand finger – you'll hear the note 'wobble.' You can hear this on the CD.

The other way to play vibrato is to shake your finger from side to side on the string. This method derives from the world of classical music and is used by violinists and other members of the string section. It's particularly effective on a fretless bass. I've played it on a fretless on the CD so you can hear the full effect.

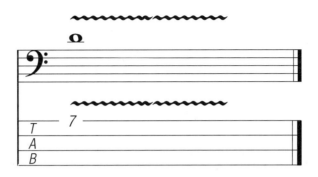

String Bending

String bending is very popular with guitarists and bassists, and it's one of the most expressive phrasing tools you have available. Bending the string can be used in place of a hammer-on to raise the pitch of a note. It can be also be used as a slurring tool. Take a look at the following notation for string bending. (These examples are also on the CD.)

In the first example you can see how the hammer-on I have illustrated could be played as a string bend. In the second example you can see the hammer-on/pull-off figure played as a bend and release.

Notice how string bends are notated – bending a note up a to the pitch of the fret above it requires an upward-sweeping arrow with a 1/2 above it. The 1/2 refers to half a tone – or a semitone, in technical terms. If we wanted to bend the note up a tone – to the pitch of the note two frets up – we would write 'full' instead of '1/2'. A bend and release is notated in the same way as a bend, but with a second downward-sweeping arrow to indicate the release.

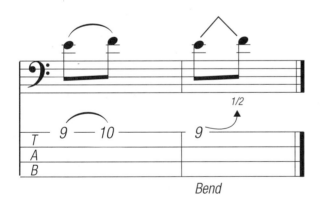

Bend

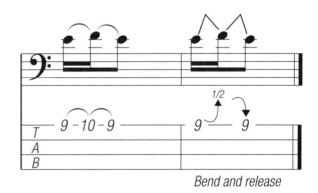

Bend and release

Phrasing Techniques In Use

In order to demonstrate the effectiveness of these phrasing tools, I've prepared an example in which I will make use of hammer-ons, pull-offs, trills, vibrato and string bends. This is notated on the next page, and you can hear it on the CD. Hopefully you'll be able to hear how effective these phrasing techniques can be.

I recommend learning to use each of the techniques described in this chapter. Not only will they enable you to play in a smoother and more graceful way but they will also help you to define your own voice on the bass. Everyone uses these phrasing tools in a slightly different way, and with a little practice you should find your own way – and your own voice.

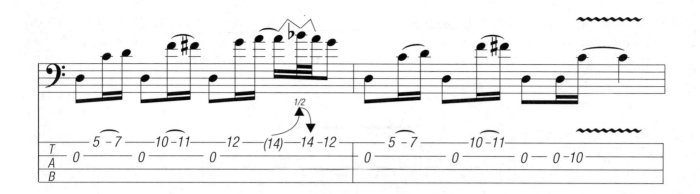

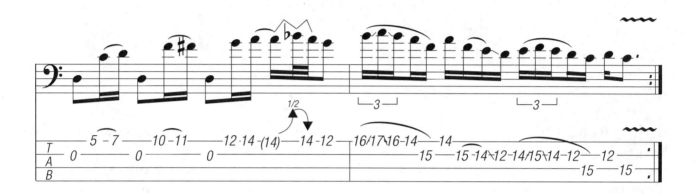

10 FINGERSTYLE

'I saw a bass player who was supporting us who used his first and his second finger, but not both at once.
So I thought I'd use both at once. Later, the same bassist came up to me and said he was influenced
by my two-finger style and I said, "Well it came from you!"' *John Entwistle, The Who*

Fingerstyle playing is probably the most commonly used method to play the bass. It's a technique favoured by many of today's greatest players from old hands like Flea and Jeff Berlin to younger players such as Chris Wolstenholme and Stuart Zender. It has been used since the inception of the Fender bass in 1951 and no doubt takes its origins from the similar technique used by jazz bassists to play the double bass. While it may not offer the immense speed that plectrum playing allows, it more than makes up for this with its many other advantages. With fingerstyle playing comes greater versatility, particularly with regard to string crossing and muting. You'll also find that it gives you more options, tone-wise.

In this chapter I'm going to take you through the various aspects of fingerstyle playing that I believe will either get you started or help you to improve on what you already have. We'll be starting with the basic stuff, such as hand position and plucking technique, before going through to some of the more tricky concepts, such as muting techniques, raking, staccato feel, ghost notes and funky 16th-note-based lines. Everything will, of course, be illustrated through examples, which are also included on the CD.

Hand Position
The first thing to consider is your hand position. Most basses have one or two pick-ups located on the body and these serve another purpose besides amplifying your playing efforts – they make a good place to anchor your thumb! It is very important to have your thumb anchored to the bass in some way when playing fingerstyle as you need a solid location to play from. (Try playing with your thumb floating in mid-air – it's much harder!) Some of the early Fender basses even featured thumb rests for just this purpose. By experimenting with your hand position, you should find that the tone you get out of the bass changes in relation to where you pluck the strings. Playing back

by the bridge and anchoring your thumb on the back pick-up (if you have one) will give you a harder, more precise-sounding tone that's great for funk lines and for playing quicker patterns. The tone towards the neck end of the bass is fuller and rounder but with less bite. Most players will alter their hand positions slightly depending on what style they are playing.

It's important to maintain a comfortable angle in your arm when playing fingerstyle. It can be all too easy to bend your wrist over the edge of the instrument when you play, but this can lead to all manner of wrist-related maladies including carpal tunnel syndrome. The best advice I can give you is to try to maintain a smooth angle through your arm and wrist, with no severe kinks. Obviously, the position of your bass on your body is also going to have a significant influence on your technique – the higher you wear the bass, the more awkward the angle in your arm will become. Wearing the bass slightly lower will ease the angles in your arm. As with all styles, you need to find the position you're most comfortable playing in and go from there.

Plucking The Strings
The next thing to consider is how you pluck the strings. You should aim to play the strings with you fingertips. This may cause some discomfort to begin with, especially if you're new to the instrument. It's possible that you'll develop some mild blisters if you overdo it, so take it slow and don't get too carried away just yet. Eventually the ends of your fingers will develop calluses, areas of hardened skin that develop as your fingers get used to doing something new. You'll probably also develop them on your fretting hand if you haven't done so already. Calluses are by no means unique to bass players – everyone who works with their hands, from builders to plumbers, will have calluses on certain parts of their hands and fingers.

It's also very important to minimise the amount of movement in your fingers as you play. Try to move the finger from the second knuckle rather than the first. There will still be movement coming from your first knuckle, but by refining your technique so that most of the action is coming from the rest of the finger you'll develop a more refined technique. Your plucking fingers should be slightly curved, with no sharp kinks – avoid bending your fingers too much at the knuckles. As with any technique, economy of motion is very important and less movement means smoother playing.

You'll also need to work on alternating your fingers in the pattern that suits you – 1, 2, 1, 2 or 2, 1, 2, 1, depending on which finger you feel most comfortable leading with.

For Exercise 1 you're just going to play eighth notes on the E string. Keep an eye on your fingers and make sure that you're alternating them properly – most beginners find that they're focusing so much on their left-hand technique that they don't realise that they're favouring one right-hand finger over another. Playing a simple pattern such as this should enable you to be looking at your plucking hand:

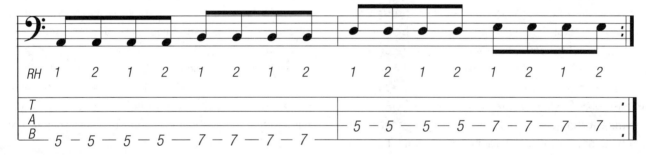

Exercise 1

You'll notice that I've indicated right-hand fingering between the staves. I've written in these numbers with the assumption in mind that you're leading with your first finger. If you're leading with your second, simply swap the numbers. It doesn't matter which you use, providing that you're alternating continually.

Exercise 2 continues in the same style, but now we move on to the A string as well:

Exercise 2

Moving to another string may present some problems for you. You may find that, when you pluck the A string, your finger is also striking the E string lightly as it comes off the A, creating a open-string hum in the background. You need to avoid extraneous noise like this at all times and keep your playing as neat as possible. Thankfully, there is a solution, one which I affectionately refer to as the 'Travelling Thumb'...

The Travelling Thumb

You'll recall at the beginning of this chapter that I talked about the importance of anchoring your thumb on the pick-up for stability. Don't worry, I'm not about to go back on what I've already told you – this remains an important aspect of fingerstyle playing – we're just going to make some modifications. When you play the E string of your bass as in Exercise 1, there's no way for you to be touching the other strings with your right hand and creating excess noise. However, when you play any of the other strings – A, D or G – you have plenty of scope for doing so. To get around this, you can move your thumb anchor according to what string you're playing. For example, if you were playing on the A string, your thumb would move from the pick-up onto the E string, muting it. This technique works for the other strings as well. As you move across the strings, try to keep your thumb anchored on the string above. This is the Travelling Thumb, and it will help to keep excess noise out of your playing.

Exercise 3 uses all four strings. As you work through the exercise, keep in mind your thumb position and be sure to move it accordingly. You should also avoid any pauses that might occur as you move your hand from string to string:

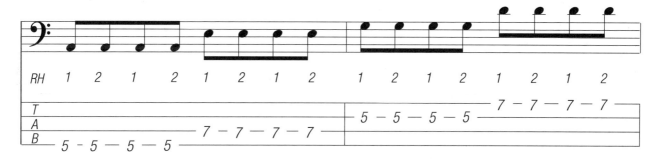

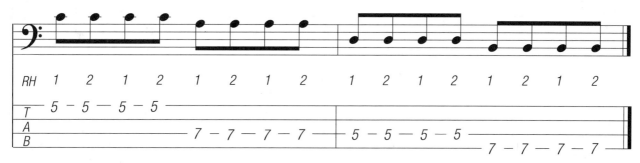

Exercise 3

This will get trickier with the more string-crossing you have to do. So far you've only jumped from string to adjacent string, but often you'll have to jump or 'skip' over a string – to play an octave, for example. In the next example, you will have to jump from playing notes on the E string to playing the D string. Be sure your thumb travels with you!

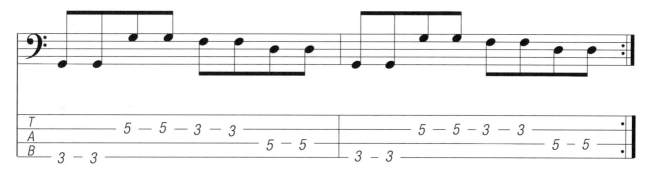

Exercise 4

This might feel awkward to begin with but it's a technique worth persevering with. It's much easier to learn this early on in your playing than it is to discover you need it later on and have to go back and retrain your hands. Trust me, I'm trying to get you into good habits here, in some cases by avoiding my bad ones! Try to incorporate this technique into the other aspects of your practice schedule – the perfect place to use it, for example, is when playing scales.

Raking

You might find it uncomfortable to alternate fingers and cross strings at the same time. Sometimes, when playing from higher strings to lower ones it can be easier to use a rake. I don't mean the garden tool, rather a technique whereby the finger that has just played the string can 'rake' back to the string below and play that string too. You can try this by playing a note on your G string and allowing your finger to come to rest on the D string. You can then play a note on the D string with the same finger. Doing this can smoothe out your technique even further. On the CD you'll be able to hear me rake across three strings with just my first finger.

Play through a descending C major scale using this technique. I've indicated a rake with an *r* before the finger number. Notice how I continue to alternate fingers after a rake:

▲ Track 50

Exercise 5

Now here's an example of a rake crossing all four strings:

▲ Track 51

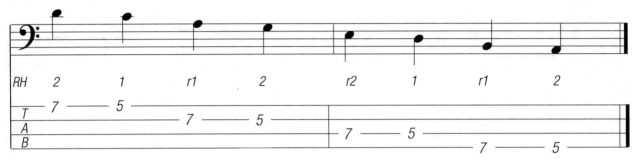

Exercise 6

More Right-Hand Muting

You might be wondering what happens if you're playing a fast passage that crosses strings frequently – it's obviously not practical for your right-hand thumb to keep jumping from one string to another. In a case such as this, I would simply anchor the right-hand thumb on the pick-up and leave it there. I would use a combination of left- and right-hand muting in this example to keep it neat. Next we'll look at another way in which we can mute with the right hand.

In all of the examples so far, the notes have been allowed to ring for their entire duration – you haven't yet played any short, staccato notes. As with all techniques, there are a number of ways to shorten and mute notes, some more successful than others. So what do we do when we want those funky, staccato 16th-note grooves? The answer lies in your right-hand technique.

Try this exercise: play through Exercise 1 again and look closely at your right-hand fingers as you play. Play the string with your first or second finger and then alternate so the

next finger plays the next note. There is no rest – as each finger touches the string, it's playing it, and the string sounds until you play the next note. Playing in this way enables you to produce long, sustained notes and smooth bass parts.

Now, to make these notes shorter, more staccato, you could apply some left-hand muting by lifting the fretting fingers off the fretboard slightly. However, it would be very difficult to play a complex bass part in this way. A simpler method is to use the right-hand fingers. Try this: as you play a note, immediately bring your next finger into position and allow it to rest on the string ready to play the next note. By doing so, you'll stop the string from ringing, shortening the note. Each finger can therefore serve two purposes: playing the string and stopping it. You'll find this to be a very useful muting tool.

Let's take a look at it in the context of an exercise. In this example I'm going to play through the same bass part twice, once with no right-hand muting and once with the muting, producing clipped staccato notes:

▲ Track 52

Exercise 7

Exercise 7 (continued)

Ghost Notes And 16th-Note Lines

Ghost notes are short, percussive notes that give a fingerstyle line a stronger sense of groove. They're used to great effect by players such as Rocco Prestia, Flea and the late James Jamerson. It doesn't matter what style you're playing in, be it funk, reggae or blues, ghost notes add character and feel to a line. To play a ghost note, let your fretting fingers up from the fretboard slightly. Doing so will prevent the note from ringing properly so that, when you strike the string, you hear a percussive note. On the CD track supporting the following example, I'll play a group of notes as normal, then a group of ghost notes so that you can hear the difference.

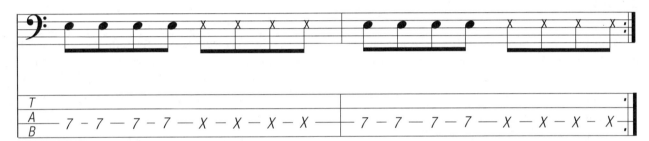

▲ Track 53

Exercise 8

Now let's incorporate some ghost notes into a groove. You should hear what a difference they make:

▲ Track 54

Exercise 9

Pretty funky, huh? Those ghost notes certainly add an extra funky and percussive element, I'm sure you'll agree. You'll also notice how I made use of 16th notes in this bass part.

Lines like this are tricky to execute flawlessly and require a thorough understanding of all of the concepts presented in this chapter. While it should be your goal to play accurately rather than fast, I must admit that lines like this are fun to play and, if played accurately, can groove really well within the right type of song. Let's take a look at how to develop 16th-note lines such as these.

Exercise 10 should help you to get started. You'll need to work on playing 16th notes with a metronome at a slow tempo in addition to working on all of the concepts presented in this chapter. Start the exercise at around 80 beats per minute and move on only when you feel completely comfortable with the tempo.

Exercise 10

The tempo that I'm comfortable with at the moment is 104bpm. I've been on this setting for about two months, so you can see that it can take a while to build up your speed satisfactorily. Don't be tempted to go too fast too soon, and remember to alternate your picking fingers continually. You should also experiment with leaving space in lines such as these.

The final example is a faster 16th-note line based on the style of the great Jaco Pastorius. This is about as relentless as these sort of lines get and you'll find it tiring for your plucking hand. You can avoid tiring your hand by making use of those phrasing techniques discussed in Chapter 9. I've used them in this exercise – believe me, it would have been much more difficult without them!

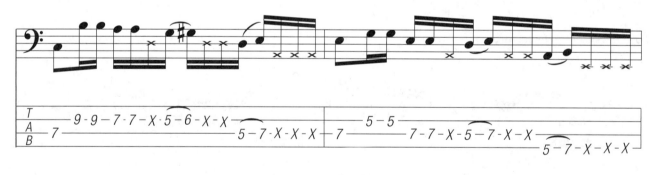

Exercise 11

Hopefully, using the techniques and examples I've shown here, you'll be able to go about improving your technique or developing it as you see fit. There's a lot of information here, and if you're new to any of these techniques you may find it slightly overwhelming. The important thing is not to be afraid of jumping in and finding out if you can swim or not. If you can, great. If not, that's where this book comes in!

11 SLAP BASS

'Any one technique is good to put in your bag of tricks to know about, because you'll never know when you'll need it. So, although I'm only a finger-plucking, regular bass-playing guy, I do the tapping and slapping now.'
Billy Sheehan, Mr Big, Niacin

Slap bass is one of the most exciting ways of playing the bass, and there are few who have picked up the instrument and not wanted to at least try it. Besides sounding very funky, it's visually impressive and still as popular today as it was when it was introduced 30 years ago. We currently have some fantastic ambassadors for the slap technique, and indeed for the instrument itself – I'm talking about players like Flea, Fieldy, Dirk Lance, Stanley Clarke, Mark King, Victor Wooten, Stu Hamm and, of course, the daddy of slap bass, Larry Graham.

To a beginner, taking those first few tentative slaps on the bass can be quite daunting. As likely as not, the first time you try it, it will feel awkward and clumsy, and it probably won't sound that great either! However, while slapping is a very popular and funky-sounding way of playing the instrument, this doesn't necessarily mean that it has to be difficult. Remember – just because something looks and sounds difficult, it doesn't mean that it is! I'm not saying that it's easy, just that it's not as hard as you might think. It's certainly worth remembering that even the best 'slappers' struggled with their thumbs to begin with. Perseverance with the following exercises will pay off – that's one promise I can make to you. Slap bass is one of the most enjoyable styles to learn, and I can also promise that, if you're a newcomer to the style, you're going to have a blast learning it. For those of you who are already well acquainted with the technique, hopefully there will be something for you here, too.

Many people assume that slap bass is all about the thumb when in fact success with the techniques lies in the integration of both hands. While it's almost impossible to produce a string of 16th notes with the thumb alone, by using both hands to hammer out rhythms it's possible to produce twice the number of notes with half the effort. I always liken this technique to drumming on a tabletop with my hands. It's quite easy to do, and pretty much everyone can already do it. By applying that same technique to the bass, you can come up with some very funky sounds indeed.

There are three elements to playing slap bass. The first two – the thumb and the left hand – I've already talked about. The third element is the first or second finger of the right hand, which is used to 'pop' the string. Over the course of this chapter, we'll look at each element and learn how to apply it to the slap style. Hopefully, by the time you reach the end of the chapter, you'll have all the ammunition you need to start creating your own lines.

Before we get started, we should look at how the slap technique is notated. In each of the examples I've written the slap guides between the two staves. It's very simple: *t* means thumb, *lh* means left hand and *p* means pop, with the first or second finger.

The Thumb

We'll start in the most obvious place, with the thumb. I always advise my students to give some thought about the way in which they slap the string. This is affected mainly by the position of the bass on your body. For example, if you wear the bass low when you play, your slap technique will be very different from how it would be if you wore it higher. Consider the contrasting styles of Flea, who wears his bass low, with that of someone like Mark King, who wears his bass quite high. Flea slaps with his hand at a right angle to the string whereas Mark has his arm parallel to the strings. Both methods work and it's down to you, the player, to decide which works best for you. Personally, I prefer to wear the bass in approximately the same position as it would be if I was seated. As discussed in Chapter 5, this enables me to maintain the same angles in my arms and wrists whether I am sitting or standing, so there's minimal difference to my technique whichever I'm doing. By doing this, I'm also able to keep my thumb parallel to the strings, which makes striking the other strings besides the E a lot easier.

To begin with, try slapping the string with the side of your thumb, on the knucklebone, and aim for just over the last fret on your bass. As you strike the string, it's important to keep a degree of flexibility in the wrist, as relaxation will enable your thumb to bounce. This is very important in the slap sound.

In Exercise 1 we're simply going to strike the E, A and D strings of the bass. If you're wondering why you're not slapping all of the strings, it's because you rarely have to slap the G string at all. Usually, this one – and frequently the D string – will be popped by the first or second finger.

Exercise 1

You'll probably find it trickier to hit the A and D strings, as you'll have the E and A strings in the way. Remember what I said about keeping your thumb parallel to the strings – this should help you to hit the string that you want. Once

you have the fundamentals of this technique under your belt, I recommend a little 'target practice', practising hitting each string in turn as accurately and cleanly as possible.

Try this with fretted notes as well, as shown here:

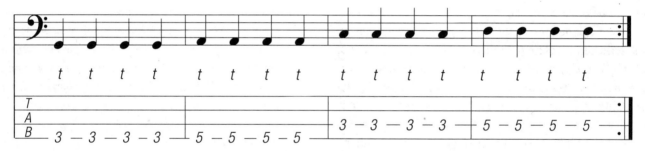

Exercise 2

The Left Hand

The left hand is equally important in the slap bass style and not just for those funky 16th-note rhythms. As I've already mentioned, it also plays a valuable part in muting. Try slapping a G on your E string. Now lift the left-hand finger slightly after you've struck the note. The note should stop. This is a standard muting technique and is used in many styles of playing. It is, however, a very useful part

of the slap style, hence its inclusion in this chapter.

In the next example I've notated a simple eighth-note bass line. By using the technique I've just explained, you can maintain a more 'staccato' feel and play a tight eighth-note groove. You can hear me applying this technique on the CD.

Here's the same line from Exercise 2 with the muting applied to it:

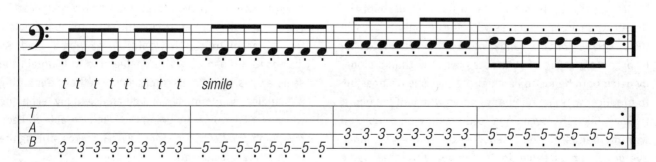

Exercise 3

Once again, refer to the CD if you're in any doubt. If you wanted to play long notes rather than staccato notes, obviously you could simply leave your fingers in place without performing any muting. Although in this instance I've added staccato marks (those little dots below each note), this is not always written in slap notation and is frequently left to the discretion of the player.

The left hand is also responsible for creating ghost notes. By slapping the string with the left hand in the correct place you can create a ghost – or 'dead' – note that will add a percussive effect to your playing. This can be a tricky concept to grasp, but all you need to do is slap

your fingers against the strings to create a 'thud'. You do, however, need to ensure that the ghost note is actually a ghost note and doesn't have any kind of pitch – hitting the strings too hard will result in a fretted note.

You also have to be careful not to play any unwanted harmonics. I've found that the best place to hit the string is roughly over the sixth fret. This fret doesn't have a strong harmonic, whereas frets 5 and 7 do. Once again, listen to the CD if you're in any doubt.

The following exercise requires you to play a slapped note with the thumb, closely followed by a dead left-hand slap:

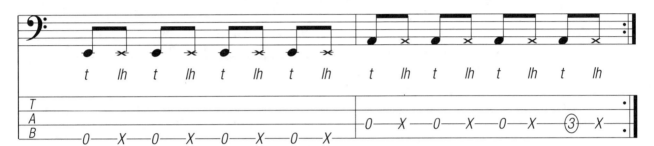

Exercise 4

Now try something a little faster. Imagine slapping out a 16th-note pulse with your hands on the tabletop. The next

exercise follows that principle, since you'll be alternating between thumb slaps and left-hand slaps.

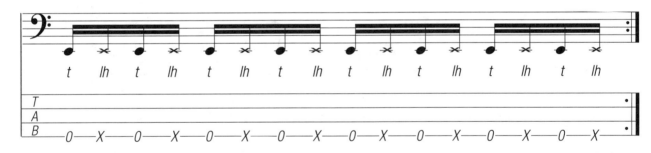

Exercise 5

Sounds pretty tricky, I'm sure you'll agree, but the principle is very simple.

You can also play ghost notes with the thumb, simply by slapping the string as you would with any note but

muting the string with the left hand. By combining ordinary slapped notes, left-hand slaps and slapped ghost notes together it's possible to produce patterns like the one in the following exercise:

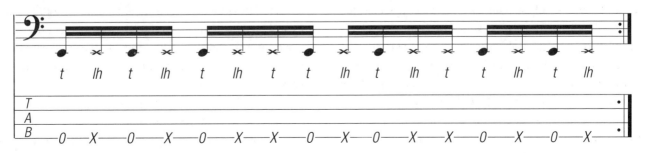

Exercise 6

Things are starting to sound funkier now – it's time to add the final element to our slap-bass arsenal.

The Pop

By using the thumb and left hand in the combinations previously illustrated, we're already able to come up some rather convincing slap lines, but an integral part of the style is the popped notes that add that final bit of funk. These are played with either the first or second finger of the right hand, it doesn't matter which. In fact, it's quite useful to be able to use both, as they will come in useful for some of the more advanced slap techniques. Try hooking your finger just underneath the G string and pulling the note. Try not to use too much of your finger – you really need to pluck only with the end to produce the desired tone. Do this quite aggressively and hopefully you'll produce the same sound as that demonstrated on the CD.

Popped notes aren't much use on their own and need to be used in context with some slapped notes. A popular choice is the octave above the note you've already slapped. Try the following exercise, which mixes the two in a simple eighth-note line:

▲ Track 67
▲ Track 68

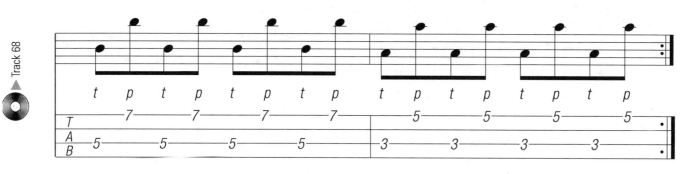

Exercise 7

By applying the muting technique discussed earlier in the chapter, you can make this sound funkier still:

▲ Track 69

Exercise 8

We've now covered the basic elements of the slap style. When combined with standard left-hand techniques such as hammer-ons, pull-offs and slides (see Chapter 9), we can produce lines of considerable complexity. While this is undoubtedly quite cool, a word of caution: slap bass can be quite addictive and shouldn't be over-used. Just because you can fill up every 16th note in a bar doesn't always mean that you should! There's the old saying 'less is more', and it applies strongly here. Adding space to your grooves allows them to breathe and quite often makes them more effective. That's a good bit of advice that applies to playing in other styles, too, not just slap.

The final five examples of this chapter are slap grooves I've written for you to practise. They vary in their level of difficulty, but by following the slap guides and using the information in this chapter you should be able to execute them perfectly. If you're new to the technique, take these slowly and carefully; there's nothing in these exercises that I haven't covered in this chapter. Hopefully you'll soon be coming up with lines like these on your own.

Exercise 9 is based around a figure which is repeated in every bar in a couple of different positions. You'll notice that I've notated staccato marks for the pops, but remember, they won't always be there:

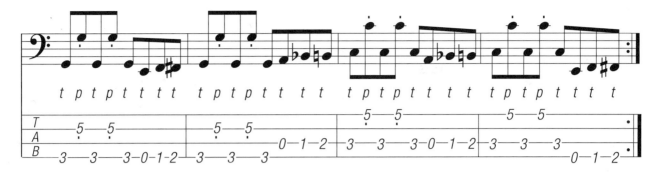

Exercise 9

In Exercise 10 you'll need to work on your popping technique to get the feel right. Watch out for the figure in the last bar:

Exercise 10

Exercise 11 contains a *double stop*, which is where two notes are popped together. To do this, pop one with the first finger and one with the second simultaneously. (See? I told you it was useful to be able to use both!) In this instance, your first finger will be popping the F♯ on the D string and your second will be popping the D on the G string.

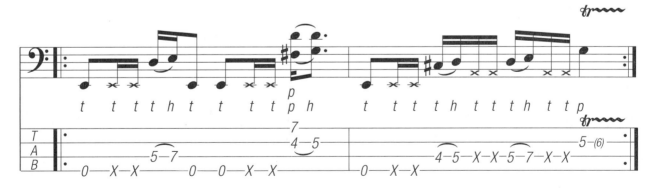

Exercise 11

Exercise 12 features some tricky hammer-ons and pull-offs. For the figure at the beginning of the second bar, you will see that a slur connects all five notes. This means that this group should sound as one fluid phrase. You might want to take this slowly to start with, especially if you're not used to hammering on and pulling off at speed.

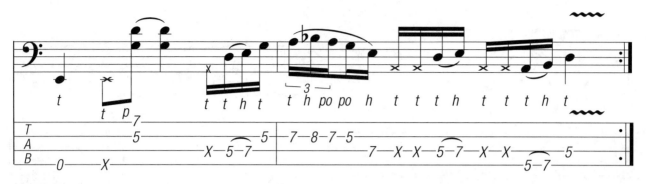

Track 74

Exercise 12

This last is a bit of a monster, but I've included it as an example of what's possible with the slap technique. Once again, there's nothing here that hasn't been covered in this chapter. Be careful with this one – there are a lot of notes and some tricky rhythms to contend with. In the first bar you'll notice that again I have included the hammer-on phrase from the previous exercise, while in the second bar we have some sliding tenths. These are played simply by slapping and popping as notated, but allowing the notes to ring into each other, creating a chordal effect.

In the third bar there is the same effect but with octaves. Remember to check out the CD if you need help with the notes or timings.

Track 75

Exercise 13

Finally, one of the most important aspects about learning something new is getting out there and listening to as much of it as you can. Check out the guys who are using this technique and see if you can work out what they're doing. Studying any of the players mentioned at the beginning of the chapter will be enormously beneficial to your slap playing, and there are many more 'slappers' out there that I haven't mentioned. For the most part, I can promise you that the grooves they are playing use only what's covered in this chapter. There are also many fine players that are pushing the boundaries of the style even further with techniques like double- and triple-popping, double-thumbing and combing slapping with two-handed tapping. These techniques are beyond the scope of this book, but maybe next time...

12 USING A PICK

'Sometimes you might want to use a pick for a more twangy sound.' *Chris Wolstenholme, Muse*

Playing the bass with a pick (or plectrum, as it is correctly named) is something that for many years has mainly been the practice of rock musicians. There are a few possible explanations for this. Firstly, playing with a pick produces a heavier, punchier sound than playing with the fingers. This is because the attack that is produced by the plastic of the plectrum striking the string cannot be reproduced with the tips of the fingers. Secondly, many rock bassists seem to have started out as guitarists, and since 95 per cent of rock guitar playing is done with a pick, it makes sense to use a pick on the bass as well. It's also a more aggressive style of playing, one that you can literally put your entire arm into – especially if you wear your bass low. You might also notice pick players wearing sweatbands on their wrists, particularly the picking hand. This is mainly to protect the skin from the constant abrasion against the edge of the bass or the bridge.

Playing with a pick has its advantages and disadvantages over fingerstyle playing, all of which will hopefully become obvious throughout this chapter.

The pick is usually held between the first finger and thumb of the right hand. As you pluck the strings, it's helpful to rest the wrist of your right hand on either the bridge or body of the bass – this provides a stable anchor point from which to play. There are many different ways to play using a pick – some bassists, for example, will use mostly downstrokes (an approach favoured by Jason Newsted of Metallica) while others use a combination of down- and upstrokes. Whether you use just downstrokes or a combination of both depends mainly on the tempo – at slow tempos it's relatively easy to use just downstrokes, but at fast tempos of 140 beats per minute upwards you're going to need both. I recommend practising using both downstrokes and upstrokes – it will enable you to play cleaner and faster.

Speed is the main advantage that pick playing has over fingerstyle. It is possible to play continuous 16th-notes at very high speeds using a pick, something that would tire the hands of even the most experienced fingerstyle player. Having said that, it's very difficult to cross strings when playing with a pick. Listen to 'Iron Man' by Black Sabbath – the closing section features a relentless 16th-note line that would be impossible to play with just the fingers, but there's no string-crossing involved. Another good example is 'Parallel Universe' by The Red Hot Chili Peppers. Their bassist, Flea, uses a pick to play a line that, while playable with the fingers, would require an even greater amount of stamina.

Let's look at some exercises that will help you to develop your pick playing. In all of following exercises I have added guides for upstrokes and downstrokes:

Downstroke = ⊓   Upstroke = ⋁

In Exercise 1 we're simply going to play eighth notes, using up- and downstrokes. Try to keep all the notes even and maintain the same volume whichever way you're picking:

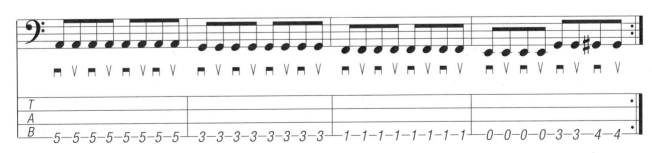

Exercise 1

Exercise 2 has a more active bass part that will require you to cross strings. Try to keep the line sounding smooth as much as possible – when playing with a pick it can be all too easy for your playing to start to sound disjointed. (You might like to find your own pattern of up- and downstrokes. The one I've written is merely a suggestion.)

Exercise 2

Now let's take a look at one of those 16th-note parts discussed earlier. For now, we'll keep to a reasonable tempo, such as 100 beats per minute. With lines like these it can be tricky to cross strings soundlessly, so make sure you have the line sounding good at a slow tempo before speeding things up.

Exercise 3

As I said earlier, the main disadvantage with using a pick is that it's very difficult to jump from string to string. Moving from one string to the next – from the E to the A, for example – doesn't normally present a problem, but if you were required to play a line that jumped continuously from the E to the D (or G), you would experience considerable difficulty. This perhaps explains why pick playing isn't used in many genres other than rock music. Rock bass parts are more static than in other genres, so energetic string-crossing is rarely required. A style like disco, however, is likely to feature bass parts that jump around, and it's therefore unlikely that a bassist playing disco would use a pick.

On a closing note, it's interesting to observe that many of the bassists from the evolving nu-metal scene are fingerstyle players who also tend to wear their basses higher up than the average rocker. It's possible that, as amplification has evolved – and since most basses now have active electronics – bassists are able to get a good, punchy sound without needing to use a pick. The recent surge in popularity of the slap technique may also explain this. As a fingerstyle player, it's easy to switch between slap and finger playing, although it's not as easy to switch between pick and slap playing!

At the end of the day, the kind of music you as an individual enjoy playing is going to dictate your style of playing. It's always worth remembering, however, that there's no reason why you can't learn both. It certainly helps to be versatile!

13 SIGHT-READING

'Because I had good reading skills, a lot of my work was in theatres, or doing TV and radio sessions.
I have to admit to playing on more than my fair share of cruise ships, too!'
Dave Swift, bassist with The Jools Holland Rhythm And Blues Orchestra

There's an old musicians' joke that goes something like this: 'Question: How do you get a bass player to shut up? Answer: Put some sheet music in front of him!'

Actually, I think the joke was originally about a guitarist, but we bassists are frequently the butt of it, too. Whatever the case, it remains a fact that many bass players can't read music and are petrified by the very concept of it. But reading music (like learning theory, scales and all the other 'boring' things) has its uses – in fact, it has a great many uses and as such can open a lot of musical doors for you. Thankfully, this is being acknowledged more today than ever before and many bassists are taking the time to learn.

In this chapter I aim to give you some handy hints to help make you a better reader. Take note: I said a *better* reader! I'm not going to teach you to read music from scratch here; I'll just be showing you how you can be better at doing it.

If you've never read music and want to learn, I suggest that you study all of the information presented in Chapter 4, 'Notation And Tablature', and digest it thoroughly. You'll then need to do some further study of your own. You need to be intimately familiar with the bass clef – there'll be no tab to guide you in properly notated bass parts.

You need to spend time studying time signatures and learn how to play the various rhythmic groupings accurately and cleanly. You need to be comfortable playing in all 12 keys, too. You should examine as much music as you can, preferably some that you already know how to play – you can then see how it's written down. As I've already mentioned a couple of times in this book, learning how to write down music will help you a great deal when it comes to reading it.

Your Environment

It helps to be comfortable when you're reading – you don't want to be worrying about your posture or playing position, so make sure that you're seated comfortably with the music on the stand in front of you. Try to have the music stand level with your chest. You don't want it too high or low so that you have to shift position or strain your eyes to see it.

It is also a good move to sit at a slight angle to the stand so that you can see the neck of your bass out of the corner of your eye. You won't have time to look at your hands when you're reading, but good positioning means that you'll be able to flick your eyes down to the bass neck and back again without moving your head too much. No matter how well you know your bass, a point of reference can sometimes come in very handy indeed.

Make sure that you have enough light to read by. Reading by daylight is usually fine, but if you find yourself in an orchestra pit or on a theatre stage, you could be in trouble when the lights go down. For this reason, a music-stand light, available from most music shops, is a very wise purchase indeed. It will keep your music lit without being overly visible to the audience.

Absolute sight-reading is rare – most of the time you'll get at least a couple of minutes to scan through a chart before you have to play it in public. Quickly scan through it, check out potential problem areas (we'll talk more about this later) and feel free to make your own notes on the page if it will help you.

A word of advice must be offered here to anyone who is writing out their own music: write in a dark pen. Music written in pencil or coloured pen can be very difficult to read in some lighting conditions.

Examining A Bass Chart

Now let's examine a bass part that was written to be sight-read. You'll notice that I've numbered certain features on the chart – there is an explanation to each of these features afterwards. Have a thorough look at the various markings and familiarise yourself with the general layout and placement of notes on the stave.

Brand New Funk
Stuart Clayton

The first thing I would notice is that this is a nice chart. Properly printed material is infinitely easier to read than handwritten material. This is an example of a good, clear chart – be prepared to see some bad ones, too!

The following is a list of the features I would look for if presented with this chart:

1   The style and tempo of the piece are often indicated at the top of the music. It's always a good idea to know what style of music you're going to be reading!

2   At the beginning of the first bar we have our key signature and time signature. This piece doesn't throw up too many obstacles in those respects, since there's no specific key indicated and the time signature is 4/4.

3   Dynamics. You will need to understand what these various symbols mean. The '*f*' at the beginning of this piece is the Italian word *forte*, which means *loud*. Dynamics give you an indication of how to play throughout a piece.

4   Chord symbols. A chart with chord symbols is a good thing. If you come across a passage that you can't quite read, knowing what the chord is can often enable you to come up with something to fit in the meantime. If you're lucky, no one will notice, but as a rule you shouldn't use chord symbols as an excuse for bad sight-reading!

5   Repeat bars. Look out for these, and be mindful of indications of how many times to play through them. If nothing is written, you simply play through it twice. I try to mark repeats with a highlighter when I look through a chart for the first time.

6   Signs and codas. These are very important since they determine how you navigate your way around a chart – you may have to go back to a previous section and then jump to another. I would also recommend highlighting these.

7   Verse/chorus indications. These can be useful in helping you to determine where you are if you get lost. For example, when the singer starts singing, that'll be the beginning of the verse.

8   Dynamics again. There are various symbols for you to be familiar with. These arrows (➤) are accents, and they mean that you should simply accent the notes.

9   Two-bar repeats. Composers use these to indicate that two bars are the same as the previous two.

10   Indication that you should go to the *coda* (Italian for *tail*, meaning an ending section of a tune). This applies only if you've reached the point that tells you to go back to the sign. As this doesn't happen until the second page, you would ignore it the first time.

11   *Sim*. This indication means that you should continue playing in the same style. In this instance, I would continue the line introduced in the previous section over the B♭7 chord but moved up two frets.

12   Tricky passages. This one stands out as being a potential problem. If you get chance before you play, take a look at complicated phrases such as these.

13   Use of previously used material. You might recognise this line from the beginning of the piece. It was used throughout the verse as well.

14   Sign instruction. *Dal segno* is an Italian phrase meaning *go back to the sign* which you will find at the beginning of the verse. You then play through until you reach the instruction 'to coda', at which point you jump to the coda, which is at the bottom of the second page.

15   The coda. Highlight all coda directions.

16   Dynamic indicating a slight pause on the last bar.

17   Another foreign word! 'Rall' is an abbreviation of the Italian word *rallentando*, meaning *to slow down*. This is quite common at the end of a piece of music.

These points will enable you to navigate your way through a chart. I recommend that you get hold of some music and scan through it, looking out for the things mentioned above. If you have transcription books, follow the music through, see how repeats and codas are used, look out for those symbols and find out what they mean. The more you immerse yourself in printed music, the better you'll get at reading it.

14 USING YOUR EAR: AURAL EXERCISES

'I think sometimes it's better when you don't have everything at your fingertips. I had to struggle because I didn't have the visual. I heard some cool stuff and then I had to go home and figure out how they did it, and while I did it I ended up making mistakes and finding something else on my own.' *TM Stevens*

It's not often acknowledged but developing your ear is crucial to your development as a bass player. Many musicians will spend years honing their technique but few will devote time to training their ears, which are assets almost as valuable as their hands. Unquestionably, musicians who can use their ears effectively to help them to determine melodies and chord progressions quickly and accurately will find themselves in more demand than those whose ears are less developed. If you've never even thought of training your ears up, it can be quite a daunting prospect. It can also be difficult to know where to start. The subject of ear training is a complex one and is deserving of a book in itself, but to help you get started I've prepared some exercises that should point you in the right direction.

Exercise 1 determines whether you can sing a note that you hear. To do this, play a note on your bass and then sing it to yourself. Don't be embarrassed to sing if you haven't tried it before – you don't need to sound like Bono, you just need to be able to pitch the note you hear with a little accuracy!

On the CD you'll hear ten notes played on the bass. There will be a space after each note for you to sing the pitch back. You should find this fairly straightforward but, if not, keep

practising until you can do it. You'll need to be able to do this before moving on to any of the other exercises.

Hopefully you can play a major scale – if not, it's back to Chapter 6 for you! Assuming that you can, you can start off simply by singing through a C major scale as you play it. Play slowly, giving yourself time to really listen to the note before you sing it. Speed isn't an issue here, but accuracy is. On the CD, I've played a slow C major scale to demonstrate **Exercise 2** – try to sing along.

When you are happy that you can do this, try using a different major scale – you shouldn't find it any more difficult. If some of the notes are out of your comfortable singing range, feel free to sing them up or down an octave as necessary.

Once you can get through Exercise 2, we can start to make things a little trickier. In **Exercise 3** we're going to play the first note of the scale and then sing the next without playing it, and so on. This isn't as difficult as it sounds, I promise you. If you can recall the old song 'Doh-Ray-Me', you should be able to hear what the next note should be. If you're feeling shy at this point, I suggest that you wait until everyone is out of the house before you start warbling! Here is the exercise written out.

Exercise 3

On the CD I have played the scale and left out every other note. Try to sing the appropriate note in the gap that I have left.

By now you'll probably have the sound of the major scale fairly well fixed in your mind. In the next exercise, play the first note of the scale and then sing the rest

without playing it. Scary? I suppose it is. Remember not to worry if your singing isn't up to much. Even if you don't hit the note accurately straight away, as long as you can hear that it's wrong and correct it accordingly, you're well on your way to achieving success with your ear training:

play   *sing* _

Exercise 4

Intervals

The next step is to practise singing any other note in the scale after hearing only the root. For example, staying in the key of C, imagine playing a C and then singing the note G, five notes further up the scale. The distance between two notes is referred to as an *interval*. Those of you preparing to run screaming from the building, stay with me! I'm going to show you a commonly used method that will help.

All the intervals we're going to look at in this chapter occur within the major scale – they are known as *diatonic intervals*, which literally means that they belong to the scale. Each interval has name, depending on its distance form the root note. In the key of C, the names are as follows:

C–D	major second
C–E	major third
C–F	perfect fourth
C–G	perfect fifth
C–A	major sixth
C–B	major seventh
C–C	octave

To sing a perfect fifth, you'd play the root (C) and then sing the G above, which the chart tells you is a perfect fifth away.

I said there is an easy way to do this, and there is – you can learn intervals by association with music you know. For example, by singing the first two notes of 'Twinkle, Twinkle, Little Star', we're singing a perfect fifth, C to G:

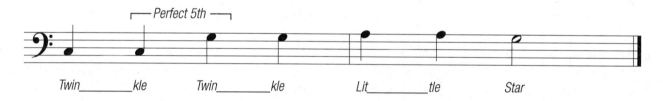

Twin_____kle   *Twin_____kle*   *Lit_____tle*   *Star*

If you can think of a well-known tune for each interval, you should be able to hear what the note should be in our head before you have to sing it. Using this method, you should find that singing intervals is well within your grasp. Try playing each interval on your bass and finding a song or melody that begins with those two notes. As another example, I like to think of the old hymn 'While Shepherds Watched Their Flock By Night' for a major third

With this in mind, try to sing a major third, as shown in Exercise 5:

play   *sing*

Exercise 5

Practise singing these intervals once a day. It certainly would do no harm to build a little ear training into that practice schedule we discussed in Chapter 5!

Further Study

To expand on what you have learnt, you also need to tackle minor scales. If you don't know how a minor scale should sound, go back to Chapter 7. You can apply the same exercises to learning the intervals within the minor scale, although this time there will be some different ones as well as the ones you already know. Again, the key is to learn them by association: try to imagine a well-known song that features those two notes next to each other and use this as a point of reference.

As I mentioned at the beginning of the chapter, these exercises really do constitute the tip of the iceberg. To further your ear development, I recommend getting a book devoted to the subject or a music teacher to help you. That said, what has been presented in this chapter should form an excellent basis for your ear training.

15 USING YOUR EAR: TRANSCRIBING

'I played bass in my room for 14 hours a day for four years and transcribed every little score from Stanley Clarke, Level 42, Jaco, George Benson and Toto, every kind of music, to become a great musician.' *Pascal Mulot*

Transcribing other bass players' lines is a valuable part of your ear training. I enjoy transcribing, and I do a lot of it, but I often meet players for whom the idea of working something out for themselves sounds nightmarish, and it shouldn't be this way.

Part of the problem lies in the fact that we as bass players are becoming more and more spoilt by the various teaching materials available. Very often these days you'll be able to walk into a music shop and pick up a transcription book of an album by your favourite artist. Guitarists have enjoyed this luxury for much longer than we bassists, but we're starting to catch up. We've never had it so good, and learning your favourite song has never been so easy. But all the while that we're getting books, videos and DVDs to teach us, we're being encouraged to be more and more lazy. Part of the enjoyment of learning your favourite piece comes from having figured it out by yourself. If you've ever sat down and worked out a difficult piece, you'll know how good it feels to get it right finally. But even more important than your sense of satisfaction is the fact that, in transcribing it yourself, you're using your ears and, in doing so, training them.

As a bass player, you're seeking to find your own voice on the instrument. The best way to do this is to absorb as much music as you can and learn from players that you admire. Transcribing other bass players' parts helps you to learn their styles, their note choices, and encourages you to think in new ways. When you transcribe a lot of material by the same artist, you'll get into their mindset – you'll start to make accurate guesses at how things were played or conceived.

Transcribing and learning from a wide variety of bassists, each of whom play in differing styles, will do wonders for your playing. To craft your own style, you must first assimilate the styles of others. It all sounds very *Star Trek*, but it's a fact. Jaco would never have sounded like Jaco had he not spent years learning soul and Motown tunes,

assimilating the work of Jamerson, Jerry Jemmot, Duck Dunn, transcribing Charlie Parker's sax lines and learning and studying melodies.

Hopefully, at this point you're nodding your head and seeing the value in what I'm telling you. In the next section we'll take a look at some of the techniques we can use to transcribe our favourite bass part.

Reading Music

It helps a great deal if you can read music, as it stands to reason that if you know how to read something you should be able to write it down. I learnt to read by learning to write music, so I guess I took the backwards approach! However, being able to write out your transcriptions in notation doesn't mean that you have to. I'll often use a combination of notation and tablature – essentially tablature with rhythms attached. The benefit of doing so means that I'm able to notate rhythms and represent the easiest fingerings and note placings in one go.

Speeding It Up

Now, you might be thinking that there can be no benefit whatsoever to speeding up something you're transcribing. After all, speeding it up will only make it harder, right? Wrong – at least partly. Speeding a song up allows the bass part to 'pop' out of the mix. I use this technique a lot on tracks where the bass part is buried in the mix. Go ahead and try it and you'll see what I mean. Find a tape player with a high-speed dubbing facility, preferably an old one you don't mind messing about with. Put a blank tape in the record deck and your song in the play deck. Record the track on high-speed dubbing – you'll hear the bass jump out of the mix. (Note: If you don't want to waste a blank tape, you can sometimes fool old tape machines by manually depressing the recording tabs inside the record deck.) Besides giving a more audible bass part (albeit with Chipmunks-style vocals attached), one of the benefits of doing this is that the speeded-up track sounds roughly an octave above the normal pitch of your bass. You may have to make some minor tuning adjustments to your bass but I'd be surprised if it varied more than a semitone. This technique is best used for tracks that have relatively simple bass lines, and if they're too fast for you to play, you should be able to hum what you hear and then translate this to your bass.

This technique can also be demonstrated by playing a 45rpm record at 75rpm.

Slowing It Down

In the days before digital technology, I would slow tracks down by using karaoke machines or four-track recorders and then detune my bass appropriately. It worked, but it was frustrating. These days we don't have to do that, as the technology exists to slow down audio without altering the pitch – another of the luxuries we enjoy today, but one I embrace heartily!

You can do this yourself through a computer using the numerous bits of software that will enable you to *time-shift*, as the process is known. (Sounding distinctly sci-fi again, isn't it?) Alternatively, there are headphone amplifiers for bass on the market that also offer this feature, and even the latest version of Windows Media Player can do it. The advantage of using such a device is that what you're hearing is slower but the pitch hasn't altered. It's therefore easier for your ear to cope with and you won't need to detune your bass.

Looping

Computers can be an amazing help when you're transcribing, and no, it's not cheating to use them! I find it useful sometimes to loop a small section of the tune I'm transcribing. (Again, there are plenty of audio programs out there that will do this for you.) This means that you hear only the part you need to, around and around.

Using the same software, you should also be able to insert stop points. When transcribing, you need to be able to stop the track after you've heard the group of notes you're working out – anything you hear afterwards confuses the

issue. I've spent many years mastering my Stop/Pause-button technique, but being able to automate it is a real bonus.

Sing It Back

As I said in the last section, you need to stop the track after the note or notes you're working out. Being able to sing them after you've just heard them is just as essential. If you can sing them a couple of times, it shouldn't take too long for you to locate those same notes on your instrument.

Creative Panning

On some older music the bass is panned to one side, either completely or partially. Check out some old Beatles recordings, for example, and try isolating first one speaker, then the other. In many cases the bass and vocals will be in one channel, guitars and drums in the other. Obviously, you can use this to your advantage.

Keeping A Notepad

As I mentioned in Chapter 5, it's always useful to keep a music pad around for when you want to write ideas down. This is equally important for transcribing. I keep a large A4 pad of manuscript paper purely for transcribing music – and it doesn't take long for me to fill it up.

Transcribing A Whole Piece

In many instances you won't want to transcribe an entire song, maybe just a lick or a fill you want to borrow, but sometimes you'll need to do the whole thing from start to finish. When doing so, I recommend a little preparation. First of all, listen through, pen and paper in hand, and sketch out the structure of the song on score paper – verses, choruses, middle eight, solos and so on. Try to draw in bar lines so that you basically have a blank chart to fill in. Look out for repetition – most songs use the same format and chord progression for each verse and chorus.

As with most things, transcribing can seem extremely daunting at first, but the more you do it, the easier it will become, I promise you. Perseverance may be required, but once you can do it, you'll realise that being able to transcribe is a particularly invaluable skill.

16 CLASSIC BASSES

'Don't ever underestimate the four-string Fender bass.' *John Giblin*

In this chapter we're going to take a look at some well-known basses in the history of the instrument. You'll have heard me mention some of them in various chapters already, and this is your chance to find out more about them. More importantly, you'll be able to hear what they sound like, since each bass is demonstrated on the CD. While some of the featured basses will be specific models, others will be examples of a concept – by that I mean a fretless bass, or a five-string or graphite bass. With each different bass, you'll hear me play the same simple eighth-note line, followed by a bass part well suited to that particular instrument.

Fender Precision Bass

▲ Track 85

The birth of the electric bass as we know it occurred in 1951 with Leo Fender's Precision bass. The name is derived from the fact that it enabled players of upright basses to switch to it and play precisely in tune. Leo might not have been the first to invent the electric bass (others had previously succeeded but not achieved any commercial success), but he did invent an instrument that was close enough in appearance to the guitar to be universally accepted.

Leo's design also met with considerable success, if not straight away. The Fender Precision bass was similar in design to Leo's Telecaster, and featured a slab body and 34-inch bolt-on neck with a headstock featuring four tuning pegs in line. Leo arrived at the 34-inch scale through experimentation, having tried various scale lengths without achieving the desired effect. The Precision sported a 20-fret maple neck, single-coil pick-up, two controls and a thumb rest.

Further listening: anything James Jamerson played on.

The bass used on the recording was 1978 Fender Precision strung with flat-wound strings.

Fender Jazz Bass

▲ Track 86

The Fender Jazz bass arrived in 1960 as a better-quality – and more expensive – alternative to the Precision. A more visually appealing instrument, it sported offset horns in the style of the Fender Jazzmaster guitar, narrower string spacing at the nut, a slimmer neck, four bridge saddles and two pick-ups. With the two pick-ups came more tonal variety, and the Jazz bass featured a three-control layout. These controls were seated on a metal plate and were joined by the jack socket, mounted on the body for the first time.

The Jazz bass was slowly embraced by the bass-playing community, although many players remained faithful to their Precisions.

Further listening: Jaco Pastorius, *Debut* album. Marcus Miller, *The Sun Don't Lie*.

The bass used on the CD recording was a 1977 Fender Jazz bass.

Rickenbacker Bass

▲ Track 87

Master guitar builder Roger Rossmeisl joined the Rickenbacker company in 1954 and the company began to produce bass guitars soon after. The first bass from Rickenbacker was the 4000, which with its unusual body shape was distinctly different from the Precision. The closest similarity between the two basses is the scale length – Rickenbacker opted for a 33-inch scale neck, similar to Fender's 34-inch scale. Rickenbacker basses were also more expensive and became the first serious competition for Fender.

The 4000 was also unique in another crucial way. Whereas Fender, Gibson, Ampeg and others were building basses in two parts (body and neck), Rickenbacker built the world's first neck-through bass. This was a concept that facilitated a stronger instrument with increased sustain and note clarity. The revolutionary design, which featured a one-piece through-body neck with wood wings attached on either side, was slow to catch on, however. Of course, today many basses are built this way, particularly high-end instruments.

In 1961 the company released its new offering, the 4001. Similar in many ways to the 4000, the 4001 had two pick-ups rather than one and selected models had a split output system that enabled each pick-up's signal to be sent individually to a separate amplifier. The 4003 was released in 1979 and was a redesign of the 4001.

The most notable Rickenbacker players are Paul McCartney and Chris Squire. McCartney was given a Rickenbacker 4001S in 1966 and subsequently used it for all following Beatles shows and recordings, including the legendary *Sgt Pepper* album. Chris Squire of the British prog band Yes also used a Rickenbacker almost exclusively and did much to further the popularity of the manufacturer.

Further listening: The Beatles, *Sgt Pepper*, *Yellow Submarine*; Yes, *Close To The Edge*.

The bass on the recording is a 1977 Rickenbacker 4001.

Hofner 500/1 Beatle Bass

Hofner, established in the 1800s, were known for building violins, but by the 1950s were attempting to gain a foothold in the bass market. Their bass, known commonly as the 'Hofner violin bass' was based on the appearance of a violin and may have been influenced by an early unpopular Gibson bass, the EB-1. It's likely that the efforts of Hofner would have gone unnoticed if not for Paul McCartney purchasing one. From the beginnings of The Beatles until 1966, Paul used the Hofner 500/1 violin bass exclusively. His status in the world's biggest band brought unrivalled attention to the instrument, which became known as 'the Beatle bass'.

Further listening: The Beatles, *Help!*, *A Hard Day's Night*.
The bass on the recording is a 1964 Hofner 500/1.

Fretless Bass

Many people think that fretless-bass history began when Jaco Pastorius tore the frets out of his Fender Jazz '62 and stunned the world with his 1976 debut album. In fact, the history of the fretless bass goes back at least another decade. In 1966, Ampeg released their AUB-1 bass, the first fretless bass guitar, inspired by the upright bass and an attempt to capture part of the upright sound on an electric. This was at least partly successful, as the fretless can be made to sound almost like an upright – but even better, the fretless has a distinct and rather beautiful voice all of its own. Early users of the fretless were Rick Danko of The Band and Boz Burrell of King Crimson and Bad Company.

Further listening: Jaco Pastorius, 'Donna Lee', 'Continuum', 'Havona', 'A Remark You Made'; Gary Willis, *Everlasting Night*; Marcus Miller, *True Geminis*.

The bass on the recording is a Bass Collection fretless.

MusicMan Bass

The MusicMan company was set up in 1975 by ex-Fender employees Tom Walker and Forrest White, who enlisted the help of Leo Fender to design a new bass guitar. MusicMan basses are distinctive in both tone and appearance, with

a body shape that is similar to the Fender design, an oval scratchplate, a single pick-up and three-plus-one tuning-peg arrangement. They were also the first mass-produced basses to feature active circuits. These basses became a classic and are still produced now, although Leo left the company in the late '70s to form G&L with George Fullerton.

Famous users of the MusicMan include Flea, Pino Palladino, Louis Johnson and Tony Levin.

The bass on the recording is a 1978 MusicMan Stingray.

Five-String Bass

Since the 1960s, bass players and luthiers alike have tinkered with the design of the bass, attempting various five- and six-string versions. Fender produced a five-string bass with a high C string in 1966. The instrument had only 15 frets and was met with indifference by the bass-playing public.

The most important development in the history of the five-string bass occurred in the mid '70s, when session bassist Jimmy Johnson bought a five-string bass from Alembic.

Further listening: The Red Hot Chili Peppers, 'Funky Monks', 'The Righteous And The Wicked'; Gary Willis, *No Sweat*, 'Liquefied'.

The bass on the CD is a Lakland Skyline SS-02 Deluxe.

Eight-String Bass

An eight-string bass may sound like something from a bassist's nightmare, but the name is misleading. In actual fact, an eight-string bass is a four-string with an extra, thinner string situated underneath each regular string.

Swedish company Hagstrom developed the first eight-string bass in 1967. Since then, many other luthiers, including Alembic, Washburn and Zon, have produced eight-string basses.

Further listening: John Paul Jones, *The Sporting Life*, *Zooma*; Pearl Jam, 'Jeremy'.

The bass on the recording is a John Gibson Custom.

Graphite Bass

Towards the end of the 1970s, various companies were experimenting with using graphite as a wood substitute for bass necks. The first of these was Alembic, whose engineer Geoff Gould had worked for an aerospace company that used graphite in the production of satellite components. Realising the benefits the strong but light material could have for bass construction, Gould and Alembic assembled a bass with a graphite neck. The result was a stronger instrument and a neck that had a more even tone than wood, with fewer dead spots. Their first graphite bass was quickly sold to John McVie of Fleetwood Mac.

Further listening: Michael Manring, *Unusual Weather*.
The bass on the recording is a Status Series 1.

Track 88

Track 89

Track 90

Track 91

Track 92

Track 93

17 BUYING A BASS

'You should always keep your first bass.' *Chris Wolstenholme, Muse*

Whether you're buying your first bass, upgrading to a better model or having a bass custom-made, there are a few important considerations. In this chapter, I'll look at the three ranges of instruments – entry-level, mid-range and high-end – and try to offer some tips and advice that will help you to make a purchase.

General

Without question, you should try a bass before you buy it. If you're a complete beginner, you may wonder what possible benefit trying a bass can have, since you might not be able to play anything! Nevertheless, it's important to sit with the bass and hold it, see how it feels, perhaps try some different models and compare them. Here's a list of general things to look for:

- Good balance. The headstock on some cheaper basses will dive straight towards the floor when you let go, which means that you'll be forever holding the bass up, having to work harder to play it.

- Weight. A bass that's too heavy is going to put strain on your back if you wear it while standing for too long. More and more bassists are realising the importance of a light, comfortable instrument that isn't going to ruin their posture.

- A smooth, comfortable neck, with no sharp fret ends that might hurt your fingers

- Good construction, with a smooth, unblemished finish.

- Most importantly, how does it sound? Where possible, you should also play through your preferred brand of amplification, even if that means taking your own amp into the shop.

Entry-Level Instruments: £100–£350

So, you've decided to play the bass guitar. Now all you need to do is buy one. It's possible to buy an entry-level bass guitar for as little as £100, but it's often worth spending a little more if you can. Obviously, the more you spend, the more you get for your money – and generally speaking, buying a bass isn't going to require you to sell a kidney! Basses in the low-budget range are getting better all the time, and it's now possible to get your hands on a very nice instrument for your money. More and more basses are now available with active electronics, something that used to be the domain purely of mid-range and high-end instruments, and where possible you should get a bass with an active circuit. Some basses also allow you to switch between active and passive modes.

Also, just because you're buying an entry-level bass doesn't mean that it can't look good. As the bass grows in popularity, more and more manufacturers are building instruments that are not only affordable but look good, too.

As far as construction goes, many basses in this range are made out of basswood, which is a commonly used wood in musical instrument manufacture due to its availability and stability. Alder is another common choice and is also used in the construction of higher-spec basses. It's always a good thing if the bass has a finish that allows you to see the wood grain, since that will mean that it's not made out of plywood. Don't laugh – some low-range basses are made of plywood and then painted and lacquered to disguise the fact.

Most necks are made from maple and fingerboards from rosewood, both of which are perfectly satisfactory choices. In this range you'll find that all of the instruments will be mass-produced, assembly-line basses. This is by no means a bad thing, since it keeps the cost of the bass down to a minimum.

Some excellent entry-level basses are made by Cort, Tanglewood, Peavey, Yamaha and Squier (by Fender).

Mid-Range Instruments: £400–£1,200

I've called this category the 'upgrade bass', as this is the sort of money you're likely to spend on your second instrument.

By now you'll probably have been playing for a couple of years, long enough to decide that it's definitely something you want to do and therefore worth spending a bit more money on. The term 'mid-range' is quite a loose one, since the price range is quite large – it's sometimes better to think of basses as lower mid-range and higher mid-range.

Either way, once you've decided to upgrade to a better bass, or even start with a mid-range bass, you have a few more options. There are now many companies renowned for building high-spec basses that are offering mid-range instruments in an attempt to reach what is without a doubt the biggest slice of the bass market. You'll find that active electronics are commonplace within this price range and through-neck designs are available – even from the lower end of the range. There are also considerably more options wood-/finish-wise than before.

Construction-wise, basses are made from a larger number of wood types, such as alder, poplar and ash. You'll also see more exotic woods like mahogany being used as strips in neck 'sandwiches', where the neck (a through-neck) is constructed of strips of different wood types. This looks very attractive and begins to appear more towards the upper end of the mid-range market.

Some recommended basses in the lower part of the mid-range are made by Yamaha, Cort, Bass Collection, Aria, Ibanez and Fender, most of whom also manufacture basses in the upper mid-range as well. In the upper mid-range we have Warwick, MusicMan, MTD and Status.

High-End Instruments: £1,200+

I've called this category the 'dream' category, since for many people, when they buy a high-end instrument, it's one they regard as their personal holy grail of basses, and one they will keep hold of.

This category again divides into a couple of subcategories. Firstly, you'll be able to walk into a shop and buy a high-spec bass straight off the wall. These basses will be built by well-known and well-established companies able to produce instruments in larger numbers than independent luthiers. You'll find that, if the bass you see isn't exactly what you want, there will usually be a full range of custom options available, including different colours and finishes, string configurations, hardware and pick-ups and electronics.

In the high-end category we also have instruments built by independent luthiers. These will be instruments built by very skilled craftsmen able to produce stunning woodworking and instruments of exceptional and personal quality. You won't see quite so many of these in the shops, since for the most part each instrument will have been produced for a specific customer.

Talking to an experienced luthier you can choose your options from the outset, by specifying exotic woods for body, neck and fingerboard, colours and finishes, and custom options – even some that you've thought of yourself.

Basses in this range will certainly feature more exotic wood choices, such as swamp ash, birdseye maple and ebony. Having a bass custom built is without a doubt a very desirable route to take, but one that could mean you having to lose that kidney I mentioned earlier!

Basses in this range include those by Yamaha, Alembic, Status, Zon, Tobias, Sei, GB, Ken Smith, Pedulla and Fodera.

Summing Up

At the end of the day, when buying a bass, there are just a few simple questions to ask yourself.

First of all, does it sound good? If so, that's the first and most important thing out of the way. Some people will buy a low-range bass and play it forever because they love the way it sounds. Don't feel pressurised into spending more money than you think is necessary.

Second, does it look good? This is not nearly as important as how it sounds, but at the end of the day we all like basses that inspire us and look like they want to be picked up and played. The third and final question is 'Do you like it?' If the answer is yes, and you can afford it, then the decision could be as simple as that!

18 RECOMMENDED LISTENING

'Each player to me represents a certain style of playing that does not get old and dated, but is rather something I want to stay in touch with and not forget.' *John Myung, Dream Theater*

At various points throughout this book I have urged you to go out and listen to some of the masters at work. By immersing yourself in great bass playing you will learn to become a better player yourself. As I'm a helpful chap, I have compiled a list of bass players and songs which I believe to be recommended listening. Don't worry if I haven't mentioned your favourite player – if I included all the players I liked, this chapter would probably constitute a book in itself! They might not all be your particular cup of tea, but they're all world-class bass players and songs. Enjoy.

Classic/Soul/Motown
Paul McCartney
With the Beatles and later with Wings and as a solo artist, McCartney has laid down some of the most solid and melodic bass parts in history.

With The Beatles: 'Being For the Benefit Of Mr Kite', 'Lovely Rita', 'Hey Bulldog', 'Something', 'Come Together'. With Wings: *Silly Love Songs*.

James Jamerson
Throughout the 1960s and 1970s, James Jamerson's bass parts propelled most of the hit records coming out of the Motown hit factory. Jamerson was one of the first to play complex 16th-note lines, none of which ever overshadowed the other band members' contributions

Stevie Wonder: 'Uptight (Everything's Alright)', 'I Was Made To Love Her'; Marvin Gaye: 'What's Going On?'; Gladys Knight: 'Heard It Through The Grapevine'.

Duck Dunn
Duck played bass for most of the Stax soul artists in the 1960s and 1970s and also on the soundtrack for the hit movie *The Blues Brothers*.

With The Blues Brothers: 'She Caught The Katy', 'Everybody'. With Aretha Franklin: 'Think'. With Sam And Dave: 'Soul Man', 'Hold On I'm Coming'.

Francis Rocco Prestia
Rocco is one of the pioneers of the 16th-note fingerstyle technique, particularly for his use of ghost notes. Rocco has worked with soul band Tower Of Power for 30 years.

With Tower Of Power: 'You've Got To Funkifize', 'Down To The Nightclub', 'What Is Hip?', 'Oakland Stroke'.

Other notable players: Tommy Cogbill, Jerry Jemmott, David Hood, Carol Kaye.

Pop/Funk
Mark King
One of the key figures in the '80s bass movement. His work with Level 42 still makes for essential listening for any bassist.

With Level 42: 'Hot Water', 'Mr Pink', 'Almost There', '43', 'Dune Tune', 'The Chinese Way', 'Lessons In Love,' 'Running In The Family'.

Larry Graham
Widely recognised as the 'inventor' of slap bass, Graham is one player that any aspiring slap player should check out.

With Sly And The Family Stone: 'Thank You'. With Graham Central Station: 'Hair'.

Bootsy Collins
One of the funkiest bass players alive, Bootsy is best known for his work with the legendary James Brown and Parliament.

With James Brown: 'Sex Machine', 'Super Bad', 'Give It Up Or Turn It Loose', 'I Got To Move', 'Talkin' Loud And Sayin' Nothin'', 'Soul Power'.

Stuart Zender
Stuart's work on the first three Jamiroquai albums is extraordinary. A young player with a lot of ideas, his playing is funky, melodic and instantly recognisable.

With Jamiroquai: 'Too Young To Die', 'Emergency On Planet Earth', 'Music Of The Mind', 'Mr Moon', 'Return Of The Space Cowboy', 'Cosmic Girl', 'Alright'.

Sting

One of the best-known bass players of all time, Sting is always tasteful in his playing, being the master of leaving space and then finding just the right note or phrase to play.

With the Police: 'Everything She Does Is Magic', 'Bed's Too Big Without You'. As a solo artist: 'Heavy Cloud No Rain.

Classic Rock
Gene Simmons

With rock legends KISS, Gene played Jamerson- and McCartney-style melodic bass parts that were both supportive and melodic.

With KISS: '100,000 Years', 'Goin' Blind', 'Christine Sixteen', 'Plaster Caster', 'Detroit Rock City', 'Mr Speed'.

Billy Sheehan

From his days with rock three-piece Talas to bass-playing duties with Dave Lee Roth, Mr Big and his current group, Niacin, Billy's playing is always exciting and innovative. A master of the tapping style, Billy's playing with his trademark grinding distorted tone is unmistakable.

With Talas: 'Sink Your Teeth Into That', 'NV43345', 'Shy Boy'. With Dave Lee Roth: 'Yankee Rose', 'Shyboy' (again!). With Mr Big: 'Addicted To That Rush'. With Niacin: 'Do A Little Dirty Work'.

Cliff Burton

As Metallica's original bassist, Burton was a driving force in the band with his classical background and grinding tone.

With Metallica: 'Pulling Teeth', 'Seek And Destroy', 'For Whom The Bell Tolls', 'Master Of Puppets', 'Orion'.

John Entwistle

Entwistle was one of rock's first true masters, with a technique and sound all of his own.

With The Who: 'The Real Me', 'Won't Get Fooled Again'.

Jack Bruce

Bruce's playing with rock trio Cream brought an unforeseen level of improvisational yet solid bass playing which sat perfectly with the drumming of Ginger Baker.

With Cream: 'Sunshine Of Your Love', 'White Room', 'Strange Brew', 'Born Under A Bad Sign'.

Jazz/Jazz Fusion
Jaco Pastorius

Still regarded by many as the world's greatest bass player, Jaco inspired all who heard him with his funky 16th-note lines, jazz soloing, and revolutionary use of harmonics.

As a solo artist: 'Donna Lee', 'Continuum', 'Portrait Of Tracy'. With Weather Report: 'Teen Town', 'Slang'.

Stanley Clarke

Doubling on both electric and upright bass, Clarke, with Jaco, revolutionised the bass in the '70s as both a solo artist and with both Chick Corea's band and Return To Forever.

As a solo artist: 'Lopsy Lu', 'School Days'.

Jeff Berlin

Jeff is well known not only for his for his outspoken, brutally honest and thought-provoking columns in *Bass Player* magazine but also for his outstanding playing as both a solo artist and a sideman. Jeff has worked with Bill Bruford, Yes, George Benson and Al Di Meola.

With Bruford: 'Joe Frazier', 'The Sliding Floor'. As a solo artist: 'Motherlode', 'Joe Frazier Part 2', 'Dixie'.

Victor Wooten

Undoubtedly one of the true innovators, Wooten is a master of pretty much every kind of technique imaginable. Combined with strong musicality, his playing is always breathtaking.

With Bela Fleck: 'Amazing Grace'. With Steve Bailey: 'Victor's Jam'. As a solo artist: 'You Can't Hold No Groove'.

Stu Hamm

In the late 1980s, Stu was instrumental in expanding the possibilities opened up by the two-handed tapping technique. Renowned for his rendition of 'The Star Spangled Banner' Stu also holds down the bottom end for guitarist Joe Satriani.

As a solo artist: 'Country Music', 'Flow My Tears'.

Funk/Rock
Flea

Flea is probably the most popular bassist in the world today, certainly with younger players, who study every note he plays with funk rockers The Red Hot Chili Peppers.

With The Red Hot Chili Peppers: 'Higher Ground'.

Tim Commerford

Tim is best known for his funky slap and fingerstyle work with Rage Against The Machine and Audioslave.

With Rage Against The Machine: 'Bombtrack'.

Dirk Lance

Dirk's playing with rock/funk group Incubus is melodic, solid and, above all, funky.

With Incubus: 'Are You In'.

Reggae
Aston 'Family Man' Barrett

As bassist with Bob Marley And The Wailers, Aston held down the bottom end on some of reggae's best-loved tunes.

With Bob Marley: 'I Shot The Sheriff'.